Getting Ready for Special Sundays

Martin Thielen

BROADMAN PRESS
NASHVILLE, TENNESSEE

Library of Congress Cataloging-in-Publication Data

Thielen, Martin, 1956-
    Getting Ready for Special Sundays / Martin Thielen.
        p.   cm.
        ISBN: 0-8054-6021-7
        1. Worship programs. 2. Baptists--Liturgy. 3. Occasional
    sermons--Outlines, syllabi, etc.   I. Title.
    BV199.03T46 1991
    264--dc20

                                                              90-35392
                                                                   CIP

To the good people of First Baptist Church,
Augusta, Arkansas,
who graciously birthed me into pastoral ministry

Preface

Getting Ready for Special Sundays concludes a trilogy of books on worship and preaching. Like my previous books, *Getting Ready for Sunday* and *Getting Ready for Sunday's Sermon, Getting Ready for Special Sundays* is pragmatic. It comes out of my experience as a pastor and worship leader.

Getting Ready for Special Sundays was written to help pastors and music directors get ready for worship on special occasions. It contains worship and preaching ideas for twenty special Sundays. If you need usable and practical ideas for making special Sundays more meaningful in your church, this book should prove helpful to you.

Contents

Introduction

I know firsthand the dynamics of preparing for special Sundays in a local church. Before becoming editor of *Proclaim* magazine, I served as a pastor. I remember well the joys and struggles of preparing another service for Easter, Christmas, or Mother's Day.

As a pastor, I was always on the lookout for worship and preaching ideas for special Sundays. As editor of *Proclaim*, I regularly hear from readers who need help in this area. Worship leaders need practical ideas for observing special Sundays. That need led me to write this book. Before sharing specific worship and preaching ideas, I will briefly examine three dynamics of preparing for special Sundays.

The Struggle of Special Sundays

Preparing worship services and sermons for special occasions can be a grueling task. What do you say about Easter that hasn't been said a thousand times before? How can you communicate the significance of Christmas in a fresh way? What can you do for Thanksgiving or Mother's Day this year? All worship leaders struggle with these issues.

I remember seeing a cartoon on this subject. After the morning worship service on Easter, a pastor greeted his congregation as they walked out the door. A man said to this pastor, "You're in a rut, Reverend. Every time I come here you preach on the same subject."

I chuckled as I read the cartoon. It reminded me of the many folks who only attend worship on Christmas and Easter. But it also evoked a nagging concern of mine and of most worship leaders. How can we avoid a rut when it comes to special Sundays?

At least two solutions exist for this struggle. First, we need not be overly worried. I've learned to trust the innate power of special Sundays. Special days of worship such as Easter or Christmas have a spiritual power of their own. Their effectiveness doesn't totally depend on the novelty and creativity of worship leaders. Regardless of what worship leaders do, God's Spirit moves among His people when they gather to celebrate God's mighty acts on special days of worship.

On the other hand, the efforts of worship leaders are important. We cannot neglect thoughtful worship planning, especially on Sundays. A second solution for avoiding ruts on special occasions, therefore, is hard work on behalf of worship leaders. We must make a sincere effort to plan and lead meaningful and creative worship services.

The Significance of Special Sundays

In spite of the struggles, special Sundays offer opportunities for meaningful worship services. The best worship experiences I've ever participated in have been on special occasions. Special Sundays offer unique opportunities for God's people to experience significant encounters with the Living Lord.

God's people have always celebrated special days of worship. For example, Deuteronomy 16:1-17 contains a festal calendar. Instructions are given for observing special times of worship. This passage includes directions for observing the Passover and the Feast of Unleavened Bread, the Feast of Weeks, and the Feast of Booths. Jewish worship has always appreciated special times of worship.

The Christian church also developed special worship occasions. We celebrate Advent, Christmas, Easter, Pentecost, and other special seasons and days of worship. Secular holidays, denominational concerns, and local church activities also offer opportunities for significant worship services. With a little creativity and a lot of hard work, worship leaders can lead powerful worship services on special occasions. Such services play an important role in the life of our congregation.

The Selection of Special Sundays

Worship leaders must carefully decide what special days to observe. Although celebrating Easter and Christmas is a given, many other special days are optional.

Special Sundays can be divided into four categories—those from the Christian calendar, secular calendar, denominational calendar, and the local church calendar.

If we are not careful, however, almost every Sunday can become a special emphasis. For example, the denominational calendar has numerous special Sundays. I've kidded that my denomination has fifty-three special Sundays per year! Nobody could or should observe them all. The same can be said of secular holidays. Worship leaders should observe those Sundays which will best meet the needs of their particular congregation.

Through careful planning, worship leaders can select a balanced and meaningful mix of special Sundays to observe in their church. Although it's not mandatory, planning your preaching and worship a year in advance will help you prepare for special Sundays. If you are interested in annual planning, you can find concrete suggestions in my previous books, *Getting Ready for Sunday's Sermon* and *Getting Ready for Sunday*.

What follows are worship and preaching ideas for twenty special Sundays. Each chapter contains an order of worship and a sermon summary. Many chapters also contain other worship ideas and extra sermon suggestions. It is my hope and prayer that God will use this book to help you get ready for special Sundays in your church.

Part I
Special Sundays from the
Christian Calendar

1

Palm/Passion Sunday

The Sunday before Easter is called Palm Sunday in some traditions and Passion Sunday in others. Some denominations call it Palm/Passion Sunday. This Sunday before Easter can be a joyous celebration recalling Jesus' triumphal entry into Jerusalem; or it can be a somber service, anticipating the cross to come.

Either theme is appropriate; it's simply a matter of emphasis. Some churches capture the enthusiasm of the triumphal entry with processionals and palm branches. Others choose to reflect on the suffering and death of Christ. As a pastor, I often used the day to emphasize Christ's passion. If so, we focused on the suffering of Jesus and observed the Lord's Supper. Then, on the following Sunday, we celebrated the victory of Easter. The suggestions in this chapter will focus on Christ's passion.

The Worship of God

He Was Wounded for Our Transgressions

Prelude
Call to Worship . . . . . Jesus Dies On the Cross . . . . . . Michael Quoist
Solo . . . . O Sacred Head Now Wounded
Hymn . . . . Alas, and Did My Savior Bleed . . . . No. 113
Invocation
Responsive Reading No. 592
Discipline of Silence
The Lord's Prayer

He Was Bruised for Our Iniqities

Hymn . . . . There Is a Fountain . . . . No. 107
Scripture Readings
Solo . . . . Were You There?
The Lord's Supper
      The Passing of the Bread
      The Passing of the Cup

And with His Stripes We Are Healed

Hymn . . . . When I Survey the Wondrous Cross . . . . No. 111
Offering
Choral Benediction . . . . Worthy Is the Lamb
Postlude

Call to Worship

I began this Palm/Passion worship service by immediately focusing on the death of Christ. In this instance, I read Philippians 2:8, "And being found in human form he humbled himself and became obedient unto death, even death on a cross." I then read the prayer/poem, "Jesus Dies on the Cross" by Michael Quoist.[1]

Throughout this poem, the piano softly played in the background, "O Sacred Head Now Wounded." Immediately after the poem, a soloist sang the song. It proved to be a powerful introduction to a moving worship service on Christ'a passion. An appropriate devotional reading on Christ's death or selected Scripture passages (from Isa. 53, for example) could be read in place of the poem.

Another order of worship for Palm Sunday can be found on page 34 of my book, *Getting Ready for Sunday: A Practical Guide for Worship Planning* (Broadman, 1989).

Preaching Ideas

On Palm/Passion Sunday, I usually preach a sermon on the death of Christ. One example, "The Crucified God," can be found on pages 137-141 of my previous book, *Getting Ready for Sunday's Sermon: A Practical Guide for Sermon Preparation* (Broadman, 1990). The last time I led worship on Palm/Passion Sunday, however, I didn't preach a sermon. Instead, I read passages from the passion narrative in Mark and Luke's Gospels. Between segments of Scripture readings, our music director sang verses (a cappella) of "Were You There?" This proved even more effective than a sermon. The passages used for this service follow.

Were You There?

Scripture Readings and Music for Passion Sunday

And as they were eating, he took bread, and blessed, and broke it, and gave it to them, and said, "Take; this is my body [which is broken for you]." And he took a cup, and when he had given thanks he gave it to them, and they all drank of it. And he said to them, "This is my blood of the covenant, which is poured out for many" (Mark 14:22-24).

And when they had sung a hymn, they went out to the Mount of Olives. And Jesus said to them, "You will all fall away; for it is written, 'I will strike the shepherd, and the sheep will be scattered.' " Peter said to Him, "Even though they all fall away, I will not." And Jesus said to him, "Truly, I say to you, this very night, before the cock crows twice, you will deny me three times" (vv.26-27, 29-30).

And they went to a place which was called Gethsemane; and he said to His disciples, "Sit here, while I pray." And He took with Him Peter and James and John, and began to be greatly distressed and troubled. And he said to them, "My soul is very sorrowful, even to death; remain here, and watch." And going a little farther, he fell on the ground and prayed that, if it were possible, the hour might pass from him. And he said, "Abba, Father, all things are possible to thee; remove this cup from me; yet not what I will, but what thou wilt." And he came and found them sleeping, and he said to Peter, "Simon, are you asleep? Could you not watch one hour?" (vv. 14:32-37)

It is enough; the hour has come; the Son of man is betrayed into the hands of sinners. Rise, let us be going; see, my betrayer is at hand (vv. 41-42).

And immediately, while he was still speaking, Judas came, one of the twelve, and with him a crowd with swords and clubs, from the chief priests and the scribes and the elders. And when Judas came, he went up to him at once, and said, "Master!" And he kissed him. And they laid hands on him and seized him. And they all forsook him, and fled (vv. 43, 45-46, 50).

Soloist sings first stanza of "Were You There?"

And they led Jesus to the high priest; and all the chief priests and the elders and the scribes were assembled. Now the chief priest and the whole council sought testimony against Jesus to put him to death; but they found none (vv.53, 55).

And the high priest stood up in the midst, and asked Jesus, ". . . Are you the Christ, the Son of the Blessed?" And Jesus said, "I am; and you will see the Son of man seated at the right hand of Power, and coming with the clouds of heaven." And the high priest tore his garments, and said, "Why do we still need witnesses? You have heard his blasphemy. What is your decision?" And they all condemned him as deserving death. And some began to spit on him, and to cover his face, and to strike him, saying to him, "Prophesy!" And the guards received him with blows (vv. 60-65).

And as soon as it was morning the chief priests, with the elders and scribes, and the whole council held a consultation; and they found Jesus and led him away and delivered him to Pilate (15:1).

And Pilate again said to the crowd, "What shall I do with the man whom you call the King of the Jews?" And they cried out again, "Crucify him." And Pilate said to them, "Why, what evil has he done?" But they shouted all the more, "Crucify him." So Pilate, wishing to satisfy the crowd, released for them Barabbas; and having scourged Jesus, he delivered him to be crucified.

And the soldiers led him away inside the palace and they called together the whole battalion. And they clothed him in a purple cloak, and plaiting a crown of thorns they put it on him. And they began to salute him, "Hail, King of the Jews!" And they struck his head with a reed, and spat upon him, and they knelt down in homage to him. And when they had mocked him, they stripped him of the purple cloak, and put his own clothes on him. And they led him out to crucify him (vv. 12-20).

Soloist sings second stanza of "Were You There?"

And the inscription of the charge against him read, "The King of the Jews." And with him they crucified two robbers, one on his right and one on his left. And those who passed by derided him, wagging their heads, and saying, "Aha! You who would destroy the temple and build it in three days, save yourself, and come down from the cross!" So also the chief priests mocked him to one another with the scribes, saying, "He saved others; he cannot save himself. Let the Christ, the King of Israel, come down now from the cross, that we may see and believe." Those who were crucified with him also reviled him (vv. 26-32).

And Jesus said, "Father, forgive them; for they know not what they do" (Luke 23:34).

And when the sixth hour had come, there was darkness over the whole land until the ninth hour. And at the ninth hour Jesus cried with a loud voice, "E'lo-i, E'lo-i, la'-ma sabach-tha'ni?" which means, "My God, my God, why hast thou forsaken me" (Mark 15:33-34)?

Then Jesus, crying with a loud voice, said, "Father, into thy hands I commit my spirit!" And having said this he breathed his last" (Luke 23:46).

Soloist sings last stanza of "Were You There?"

Note

1. Michael Quoist, *Prayers* (New York: Sheed and Ward, 1963), 173-175.

2

Easter

The Worship of God

Christ the Lord Has Risen Today, Alleluia

Prelude . . . . O Worship the King . . . . Handbell Choir
Choral Call to Worship . . . . Fanfare for the Risen Christ
Responsive Reading
      Pastor: Hear the good news of Easter.
      People: He is not here, He is risen.
      Pastor: Jesus, our Lord, is risen.
      People: Christ is risen indeed!
      All: We worship the Lord who lives.

Raise Your Joys and Triumphs High, Alleluia

Hymn . . . . Christ the Lord Is Risen Today . . . . No. 114
The Greeting
Chorus
      He is Lord, He is Lord.
      He is risen from the dead and He is Lord;
      Ev'ry knee shall bow, ev'ry tongue confess
      That Jesus Christ is Lord.

Lives Again Our Glorious King, Alleluia

Invocation
Handbells' Musical Praise . . . . Christ the Lord Is Risen Today

Hymn . . . . Low in the Grave He Lay . . . . No. 118
Offertory Prayer
Offertory . . . . . . How Great Thou Art . . . . . . Piano and Organ duet

Love's Redeeming Work Is Done, Alleluia

Scripture Reading . . . . Matthew 28:1-10
Solo . . . . Was It a Morning Like This?
Sermon . . . . Is There Hope? . . . . Pastor
Choral Praise . . . . Fanfare for the Risen Christ
Hymn of Invitation . . . . Because He Lives . . . . No. 448
Choral Benediction . . . . Alleluia! Alleluia!
Postlude

Music

Easter is the time to "pull out all the stops" in music. If you have a handbell choir, use them. Do you have talented soloists? Let them sing. Prepare your choir for a victorious Easter anthem. Have a men's quartet sing an Easter hymn. Ask your instrumentalists to offer a special musical praise. Have a powerful piano and organ duet. The power, mystery, and victory of Easter's message is better communicated through music than through preaching. Whatever musical resources you have, use them to the fullest on Easter—the most special Sunday of the year.

Visual Aids

On Easter we celebrate the resurrection of Christ. It's a time to adorn the sanctuary with Easter lilies and banners of victory. Use your imagination. Ask the youth to make a banner. Allow the children to decorate the vestibule. Ask a women's group to make a quilt and hang it on the sanctuary wall. Put a large white cross, covered with flowers, in the front of the sanctuary. Celebrate!

Is There Hope?
Matthew 28:10

Years ago a submarine sank off the coast. As soon as possible, divers descended. They investigated the disabled ship, endeavoring to find some sign of life. At last they heard a gentle tapping. Listening intently they recognized the dots and dashes of the Morse code. The message from within the disabled ship was, "Is there hope?"[1]

We all ask that question. Behind all the fine clothes we are wearing today, behind all the smiles and songs of victory we've sung, great fears lurk. We, like the sailors in the sunken submarine, often wonder, "Is there hope? Is there hope for life and is there hope for death?"

That question lurked in the minds of the women who went to the cemetery on that first Easter. It was a dismal day. The women went to anoint a dead body—a sad and depressing task. (Read v. 1.)

We think of this story as a joyous experience. And ultimately it is. But it didn't begin with joy. It began with discouragement and depression. These women's dreams were broken, their hopes dashed. They had such high hopes—hopes fanned into flame by the miracles and teachings of the remarkable Man from Galilee. They believed He was the Messiah and that He would usher in the kingdom of God. Peace and prosperity would come for all. Justice would reign, things would be made right. But those hopes had been smothered by the execution that took place on Golgotha's hill. Their Messiah, their Jesus, their hope—was dead.

The day did not begin with joy but with depression. The day did not begin with victory but with discouragement. The day did not begin with shouts of hosanna but with dashed hopes and broken dreams.

What about your hopes and dreams today? Dreams of happiness and success. High hopes for your career and family. Maybe you feel like a woman I once talked to. She said, "I'm seventy-three years old but I feel like I've never really lived." Her life story consisted only of dashed hopes and broken dreams.

So the women walked to the cemetery—feeling dismal and depressed and expecting more of the same. They were, after all, simply walking to a cemetery. If you've seen one cemetery you've seen them all. People live, people die, and people are buried in the cemetery. Jesus lived, Jesus died, and now Jesus was buried in the cemetery. That should have been the end of the story. They would finish anointing His body for final burial and it would all be over.

As they arrived, however, strange and scary things began to happen.

There was an earthquake and an angel. (Read vv. 2-3.) Events at the cemetery turned bizarre and frightening. (Read v. 4.) Their depression and discouragement immediately turned to fear.

We know about fear. Behind our airs of confidence we are like frightened children. We fear that we are not good enough; we fear failure; we have fears about finances and our families. We fear that we may live our life and get to the end and discover, like the woman I mentioned earlier, that we've never really lived. We fear that our life doesn't make any difference. We fear that we are not loved. We fear being alone. We fear that we'll never be happy or achieve our hopes and dreams. We fear getting old, getting sick, and dying.

I remember a man from my first pastorate. He prided himself on being a self-made, self-sufficient, macho man. Nothing frightened him. He could face anything—so he thought.

One day he suffered a massive heart attack. I went to see him at the hospital. Several members of the family were visiting him. Even in the intensive care room, he seemed so confident. He made jokes and said everything was fine. But then the people left and it was just him and me. His cocksure attitude immediately left. He looked at me and with a tear in his eye he said, "Preacher, I'm scared."

Well, who's not? We live in a crazy, anxiety-filled, often-cruel, unfair, and confusing world. It's scary.

These women came to the cemetery depressed and then became fearful. We know about both. We've taken many walks of our own to the cemetery.

And yet, in the context of depression and fear, comes the message of Easter. Right there in the cemetery, in a place of death and broken dreams—comes good news. Death is not the final word. Depression is not forever. Fear does not win out.

In the midst of death, depression, and fear comes the word of God. Hear it again. (Read vv. 5 and 6.) "He is not here; for he is risen"(v.6).

And so we come again to church this Easter. We're dressed so fine and we smile so big, and we sing "Christ the Lord Is Risen Today" with winsome voices. But like frantic sailors in a disabled submarine we secretly tap out the question, "Is there hope?"

Easter says yes, there *is* hope! Hope for life and hope even for death. Easter says, "Do not be afraid."

At the end of today's service we're going to sing, "Because He Lives." That's the message of Easter. It says there is hope in life. Hope for meaning and purpose. Hope for forgiveness. Hope for God's strength to face difficult times.

And more than that, Easter tells us there is hope even in death. Four days ago I walked again to the cemetery and buried one of our beloved church members. And I read again the words of Scripture, "I am the resurrection and the life," said the Lord, "he who believes in me though he die yet shall he live"(John 11:25).

Ultimately, that's all that counts. Life is brief. Death is real. Very soon they will carry us to the cemetery. But the empty tomb and the resurrected Lord say there is hope even when we face the valley of the shadow of death.

They walked to the cemetery on that first Easter morning. They began the day feeling depressed—depression changed to fear—but fear ended in joy. (Read v. 8.)

They had been living in the shadow of Friday—the shadow of death and discouragement—the shadow of broken dreams and dashed hopes. But now it's Sunday—resurrection day. And everything is different. It had been Friday, but now it was Sunday.

Anthony Campolo tells of a special sermon preached by a black brother. The basic thrust of the sermon was this simple message: "It's Friday, and Jesus is on the cross. But that's all right, because it's Friday, and Sunday's coming." Now that message might not overly excite you. But listen to the message as the black pastor preached it.

He said, "It's Friday, and Jesus is on the cross. But that's all right, because it's Friday, and Sunday's coming.

"It's Friday, and Mary's soul is burdened. Her face is stained by the tears. Her heart is in anguish. Her son is gone. But that's all right. Because it's Friday. And Sunday's coming.

"It's Friday, Pilate and the Pharisees are strutting around like they own the world. But that's all right. Because it's Friday. And Sunday's coming.

"It's Friday. And Satan is smiling. Darkness has won the victory. Satan is the conqueror. But that's all right. Because it's Friday. And Sunday's coming."

He went on and on like this for forty-five minutes. "It's Friday, but Sunday's coming. It's Friday, but Sunday's coming." He continued time after time until his congregation was sitting on the edge of their seats. Finally he ended his sermon by shouting at the top of his voice, "It's Friday!" And then with one voice the congregation shouted back, "But Sunday's coming!"

So here we are, like sailors in a disabled submarine at the bottom of the sea. And we tap out the question, "Is there hope?"

And the answer of Easter comes thundering out again, yes, there is hope, because Sunday is coming, because Sunday is here, because Christ the Lord has risen from the dead!

Note

1. Walter Knight, compiler, *Knight's Master Book of New Illustrations* (Grand Rapids: Eerdmans, 1956, reprinted 1981), 557.

3

The Sunday After Easter

When I served as a pastor, I was a member of a ministerial support group. Although I did not follow the lectionary, many pastors in the group used the lectionary in their weekly worship services. We spent a portion of our weekly meetings, therefore, studying Sunday's lectionary reading. Although I did not often preach from the lectionary text, I enjoyed the Bible study and found it to be a good discipline.

Over the years, I noticed that John 20:19-29 was often the lectionary Scripture reading for the Sunday after Easter. John 20 tells about Thomas's struggle with faith after the resurrection. It serves as an excellent text for the Sunday after Easter.

On Easter Sunday, worship is full of joy and celebration. None of us, however, can stay at that level of victory forever. Like Thomas in John 20, we sometimes have doubts. At times, we struggle with our faith. Like the father in Mark 9:24, we often cry out to the Lord, "I believe; help my unbelief."

One year I decided to join my colleagues and use the text in John 20 for the Sunday after Easter. I developed an order of worship and sermon around the theme of belief and doubt. I used the story in Mark 9:14-29 as the worship outline, and the John 20 passage for my sermon. It proved to be a positive worship experience. The service and sermon follow.

Worship Ideas

The Worship of God
I Believe . . .

Eight days later, his disciples were again in the house, and Thomas was with them. The doors were shut, but Jesus came and stood among them, and said, "Peace be with you." Then he said to Thomas, Put your finger here, and see my hands; and put out your hand, and place it in my side; do not be faithless, but believing." Thomas answered him, "My Lord and my God!"(John 20:26-28).

Prelude
Children's Sermon
Hymn . . . . Praise to the Lord, the Almighty. . . . . No. 10
Baptism Service
Hymn . . . . To God Be the Glory . . . . No. 33
Affirmation of Faith

We believe in God the Father, Creator, Ruler of all things, the Source of all goodness, truth, and love.

We believe in Jesus Christ the Son, God manifest in the flesh, Redeemer and Lord, and ever-living Head of the Church.

We believe in the Holy Spirit, God ever-present, for guidance, comfort, and strength.

We affirm our commitment to God, and pledge anew to love the Lord our God with all our heart, soul, mind, and strength, and to love our neighbor as ourselves.

Hymn . . . . Faith Is the Victory . . . . No. 377
Offertory Prayer
Offering

Help My Unbelief

Now Thomas, one of the twelve, called the Twin, was not with them when Jesus came. So the other disciples told him, "We have seen the Lord." But he said to them, "Unless I see in his hands the print of the nails, and place my finger in the mark of the nails, and place my hand in his side, I will not believe"(vv.24-25).

Scripture Reading .... John 20:19-29
Anthem................ He Cares for Me .... Choir
Sermon .... Coping with Doubt .... Pastor
Hymn of Invitation .... Just As I Am. .... No. 187
Benediction
Postlude

Children's Sermon

At the beginning of the service, I came into the sanctuary wearing my baptismal clothes and invited the children to come forward for a brief children's sermon. I showed them my robe and even my waders! I pointed to the baptistry and told the children that we were about to observe baptism. I then briefly explained its meaning. I told them that baptism was an important event and asked them to pay close attention to the baptism service.

Baptism

Baptism is a great affirmation of faith. It is also a beautiful symbol of the gospel. It is hard to improve upon a simple baptism service. When I baptize I begin by reading an appropriate passage of Scripture and briefly explain the meaning of baptism. After the candidate enters the water, I usually say the traditional baptism words, "In obedience to the command of our Lord Jesus Christ, and upon your public profession of faith in Him as Savior and Lord, I baptize you in the name of the Father, the Son, and the Holy Spirit."

Sometimes, as I immerse the person into the water, I say, "Buried with Him in baptism, raised to walk in newness of life." After the baptism I usually offer a prayer for the person just baptized. Then I say something like, "Although we rejoice today that this one has come into our fellowship of faith, let us always remember—there is room for more."

There are many ways to enrich baptism. Some pastors light a candle for each person being baptized and say something about the light of the world. Others ask family members to participate in the service in various ways such as reading Scripture, giving a testimony, or actually standing with the candidate in the baptistry. Regardless of how you observe it, baptism is a significant event in the life of the church.

Coping with Doubt
John 20:19-29

Last Sunday we celebrated Easter. We rejoiced that Jesus our Lord is alive, that He has risen from the dead. But there are many times when we can better relate to Good Friday than we can to Easter. There are times when we experience more of the pain, suffering, struggle, and doubts of the cross than the joys of the empty tomb. Faith is not always lived out in the joy of Sunday. Sometimes faith is lived out in the pain of Friday.

The outline for today's worship service comes from a story in the Gospel of Mark. A father came to Jesus with a sick son. He wanted healing for the boy. Jesus told him healing was possible if he would believe. The father cried out, "I believe; help my unbelief!"(9:24).

Most of us can identify with that father. We do believe—we wouldn't be here today if we didn't. Yet we have times of unbelief—times of struggle and questions and doubts. We don't usually doubt God's existence. However, we do have times when we doubt His justice, His love, His fairness, His involvement in the world, and His concern for us. "Lord I believe, help my unbelief!"

Such seems to be the sentiment of the apostle Thomas, and I'd like to turn our attention to him this morning. We all have times of doubt. This story of Thomas can help us overcome our doubts.

The story begins on Sunday night of the resurrection. Jesus appeared to the disciples but Thomas was not there. When Thomas heard the reports of the resurrection he wasn't convinced. Thomas was skeptical. He wanted to believe, but couldn't blindly accept such amazing claims.

Thomas wasn't such a bad guy. Earlier in the day Mary told the disciples the same story—that Jesus was alive and that she had seen Him. But most of them didn't believe her. Like Thomas, they hadn't seen the Lord and were not convinced. As a matter of fact, lots of skepticism existed concerning Jesus' victory over death. Mark 16:10-11, Matthew 28:17, and Luke 24:41 all record doubts about Jesus' resurrection.

It wasn't easy to believe. Thomas had watched Jesus die. How could He be alive? Thomas's doubts are understandable. Thomas wanted to believe but he wanted his belief to have substance. He wanted his faith to be more than wishful thinking. He had believed and been disappointed once before. Thomas followed Jesus for three years only to see Him crucified. He pinned his hopes on Jesus only to see those hopes nailed to a tree on Golgotha. He didn't want to hope again without good cause. So, at least for awhile, he did not believe.

Then, eight days later, Jesus returned to the disciples. It had been eleven days since the cross and Thomas had been in agony throughout those days. Finally, Jesus came to help Thomas in his unbelief and he overcame his doubt. Upon seeing Jesus, Thomas cried out one of the greatest confessions of faith in the New Testament, "My Lord and my God!"(John 20:28). This—from the lips of a doubter!

This story in John 20 is a powerful passage. It teaches us some tremendously important truths about faith and about doubt. Let's review a few of these truths this morning.

Times of Doubt Are Inevitable

Thomas had just seen the cross. His hopes and dreams were killed at Calvary. We all live in the shadow of the cross at various times in our life. We all experience shattered dreams, lost hope, suffering, and pain. We all have questions about God and life which we cannot answer. Doubts about God's love and involvement in our life are bound to surface from time to time.

People who don't struggle with doubts are people who don't take their faith seriously. If we do take our faith seriously, it's inevitable that we occasionally struggle with hard questions and difficult situations. Thomas spent three years with Christ. He touched Him. He talked to Him. He heard Jesus teach with the authority of God. He saw Him perform mighty miracles. He even saw Jesus raise people from the dead. And yet Thomas still doubted. And there will be times when we will do the same. Occasional doubts are inevitable.

Times of Doubt Are Permissible

It's OK to have struggles and questions concerning our faith. Occasional doubts are not wrong. Faith doesn't mean we never doubt, question, or struggle. The Bible is full of examples of such struggles. Even Jesus felt abandoned when He hung on the cross. Doubt is not the opposite of faith but part of faith. And times of doubt have value. After we struggle with doubt we come out better and more mature, stronger than before. Tennyson was right when he said, "There lives more faith in honest doubt, Believe me, than in half the creeds."

God gives us permission to doubt. It's not wrong. We certainly don't need to spend all our time doubting and struggling with our faith, but such times will occur from time to time and that is permissible.

We Can Survive Times of Doubt

The real issue is, what can we do about it? How do we cope with questions and doubts? Our text suggests several strategies for survival.

First, we must remember the faith of our past. Surely, Thomas spent a lot of time thinking about the past three years with Jesus. He recalled moments of intense faith, moments when God had been real to him.

When God seems distant in the present and faith is hard to come by, we must remember our past faith. God has been real to us in years past and affirming that will help us in the present.

Second, we must hope for renewed faith in the future. Recalling past faith gives rise to hope. When we recall our faith of the past then we can anticipate a faith for the future. If God has been real to us in days past then it's a good bet He'll be real to us again in the days to come.

The present moment is fleeting. We may have doubts today but faith will be real again tomorrow. Thomas must have had hope for regaining his faith. If not, why did he stay with the disciples? By looking back at past faith, and looking forward with hope for future faith, Thomas was able to cope with the present moment, bleak as it was.

This strategy of recalling past faith, coupled with anticipation of future faith, is a powerful help in times of doubt. It's also evidence of deep and mature faith.

In his book, *The Screwtape Letters*, C. S. Lewis has a senior devil giving advice to a junior devil in the art of temptation. In one section, the senior devil writes to the junior devil:

> Do not be deceived, Wormwood. Our cause is never in more danger than when a human, no longer desiring, but still intending, to do our Enemy's will, looks round upon a universe from which every trace of Him seems to have vanished, and asks why he has been forsaken, and still obeys.[1]

When we try to follow God and obey His word in spite of our doubts and struggles, we are living out mature faith. And recalling past faith and anticipating future faith will help us survive.

A third strategy for surviving doubts is to remain with the community of believers. Thomas could not yet believe the news of Christ's resurrection. He agonized over his faith. But Thomas did not leave the disciples. Although he didn't have their faith, he stayed with them for strength and encouragement.

When we are struggling with doubt and questions—it's then that we most need the fellowship of the saints. Even when we feel dry and our faith is lifeless, we need to gather with the believers for prayer and worship and fellowship. None of us can live out our faith alone. Not in the good times and certainly not in the bad times. We need the strength of the church. When we hurt, struggle, and doubt, it is then that we must remain with the community of faith.

Finally, when we are struggling with doubts, we must be open for new evidence of God's reality. Thomas wanted evidence of Jesus' resurrection. He wanted to believe and looked for reasons to do so. He opened himself to new evidence of God's reality in his life.

In times of doubt we must seek the face of God. We must be open to new and fresh evidence of His involvement in our life. It may come in worship—through a sermon, song, Scripture reading, or moment of silence. It may come when we look again at the beauty of nature. Or it may come through the concern and love of a friend or family member. But when we are struggling with doubt, we need to be on the lookout for a new encounter with God.

Thomas's renewal of faith came in the upper room when he saw the Lord. He didn't, however, touch Jesus' hands and side. Thomas simply fell down and confessed his faith. We never have final absolute scientific proof of God. That wouldn't be faith. But we can find enough evidence of God's reality to believe again.

I spoke earlier about the father who came to Jesus and cried out, "I believe; help my unbelief!" All of us have times of belief mixed with unbelief. If not today, then yesterday; if not yesterday, then tomorrow. Even the apostle Thomas had times of doubt. So will we. Such times are inevitable and are permissible. And when they come, we can survive them. To do so, we must remember to: (1) Remember our past faith, (2) Anticipate a future faith, (3) Stay with the community of believers, and (4) Be open to new evidence of God's reality in our life.

It may be that some of you today are struggling with doubts. You may feel that God is far away. Like Thomas, maybe you can't experience the joy of Easter but only feel the pain of Good Friday. If so, let me encourage you to have hope. The living Lord will come again! He did for Thomas, and in God's timing, He will for you.

Note

1. C. S. Lewis, *The Screwtape Letters* (New York: MacMillan Publishing Co., 1974), 39.

4

Pentecost Sunday

Many of us in the Baptist and other evangelical traditions neglect Pentecost Sunday. We hesitate to observe it for several reasons. Perhaps our major resistance is that we don't want to be like the charismatics or the Catholics. This neglect, however, has been to our detriment.

Today's church needs to emphasize the work of the Holy Spirit. Since we usually focus our attention on God the Father and Christ the Son, we often neglect the third member of the Trinity, God the Holy Spirit. Observing Pentecost Sunday is a good opportunity to overcome this serious neglect of the Spirit.

Pentecost is recorded in Acts 2. Marion Aldridge shares some important information about Pentecost in his excellent book, *The Pastor's Guidebook: A Manual for Special Occasions* (Broadman Press, 1989). Aldridge points out that the people who gathered at the first Pentecost were in Jerusalem for the Jewish holiday called Pentecost, also known as the Feast of Weeks. This was a thanksgiving festival for the wheat harvest, commanded in Exodus 34:22. The term "Pentecost" came from the fifty-day period between two important Old Testament events: (1) the ceremony of "the barley sheaf" (see Lev. 23:9-11) during the Passover and (2) the Feast of Weeks. (See vv. 15-21.)

Rather than relating Pentecost to the harvest, the Christian calendar places Pentecost fifty days, or seven weeks, after Easter. Pentecost as a distinctive Christian holiday first appeared in the third century, though mention of Paul's observance of Pentecost is found in Acts 20:16 and in 1 Corinthians 16:8.

Aldridge points out that two great theological themes demand to be treated at Pentecost: the Holy Spirit and the church.

The following order of worship and sermon come from Acts 2. The service focuses on the work of the Holy Spirit. The sermon focuses on the church. Since the church was "born" on the day of Pentecost, it is a good time to focus attention on the church. Sermons could also be preached on the doctrine of the Holy Spirit, the gifts of the Spirit, the fruit of the Spirit, the comfort and guidance of the Spirit, etc. Don't hesitate to observe Pentecost Sunday in your church. It offers a great opportunity to teach your church about two of the greatest themes of the New Testament—the Holy Spirit and the church.

The Worship of God

They Were All Together in One Place (Acts 2:1)

Prelude
Call to Worship . . . . Sweet, Sweet Spirit . . . . No. 255
The Greeting
Doxology
Invocation

And They Were All Filled with the Holy Spirit
(Acts 2:4)

Hymn . . . . Breathe on Me . . . . No. 131
Discipline of Silence
Pastoral Prayer
Hymn . . . . Pentecostal Power . . . . No. 130
Offering

Peter. . . . Lifted Up His Voice and Addressed Them
(Acts 2:1114)

Scripture Reading . . . . Acts 2:40-47

And he testified with many other words and exhorted them, saying, "Save yourselves from this crooked generation." So those who received his word were baptized, and there were added that day about three thousand souls. And they devoted themselves to the apostles' teaching and fellowship, to the breaking of bread and the prayers.

And fear came upon every soul: and many wonders and signs were done through the apostles. And all who believed were together and had all things in common; and they sold their possessions and goods and distributed them to all, as any had need. And day by day, attending the temple together and breaking bread in their homes, they partook of food with glad and generous hearts, praising God and having favor with all the people. And the Lord added to their number day by day those who were being saved.

Anthem .... Adult Choir
Sermon .... What Kind of Church?

And the Lord Added to Their Number (Acts 2:47)

Invitation Hymn .... No. 132
  Spirit of God, Descend Upon My Heart
Benediction
Postlude

What Kind of Church?
Acts 2:40-47

Today is Pentecost Sunday. Acts 2 tells about the first Pentecost. It was a remarkable day. God's Spirit moved in a powerful and special way and the church of Jesus Christ was born.

On this Pentecost Sunday, as we look back to Acts 2 and the birth of the church, I want to share with you my vision of the church. Usually, my sermons are more focused and specific. Today, however, I want to look at the forest and not the trees. I want to share in broad strokes a description of the early church, which is the kind of church God still wants us to be today. My concern is not for us to remember a lot of points, but to catch an overall vision of this early church. Why? Because this church serves as our model, our goal to strive for. Please turn again to the second chapter of Acts, beginning at verse 40.

" And he testified with many other words and exhorted them saying, save yourselves from this crooked generation."

The first thing to note about this early church is that it was a *proclaiming church*. Peter proclaimed the gospel of the life, death, and resurrection of Jesus Christ. Evangelical Christians have long emphasized the proclamation of the gospel. That is why the sermon is at the heart of the worship service, and why the pulpit is front and center in the sanctuary.

Proclamation is a priority for me as your pastor. But let me add an important note. Proclaiming the gospel is not limited to the pastor nor to formal worship services. God calls us all to proclaim the gospel daily as we witness for Christ in our words and deeds. All Christians should proclaim the good news. This early church was a proclaiming church.

The result is seen in verse 41, "So those who received his word were baptized." They were a *baptizing church*. The church has many functions but we must never forget that a top priority is to reach people for Christ and see them baptized. They were a baptizing church.

In the first part of verse 42 we read, "And they devoted themselves to the apostles' teaching." The early church was a *teaching church*. They taught God's word, and so should we. People need to be taught the Bible.

Years ago, when ships were the only way communications could be carried from the old countries to America, people in America, anxious for news from relatives and loved ones, would assemble at the dock as soon as a mast was sighted. The moment a gangplank was thrown up and sailors began to disembark, hands would stretch out and cries would go up from the crowd beseeching, "Is there any word? Is there any word?"[1]

We need a word from God for the living of these days. So the church must be involved in teaching His word. They were a teaching church.

In the middle of verse 42 we read that they "devoted themselves to fellowship." They were a church of strong fellowship. They were friends. They cared about each other. They helped, supported, and loved one another.

God wants His church to be a church of *strong fellowship*. The church needs to be a place where we can laugh together and where we can also cry together.

A few years ago, I buried an eighteen-year-old boy who had been killed in a car accident. It was the hardest funeral I've ever done, and I've done a lot of them. But I saw my church rally around that family. They wept with them, held them, and cared for them. And they continued that kind of support for months and even years. When I see such support, I understand what church fellowship is all about.

You see, we desperately need other people. We are not self-sufficient. We are frail, weak creatures, and we need the strength of a church family. God wants His church to be a church of strong fellowship.

At the end of verse 42 we read that they also "devoted themselves . . . to prayer." They were a *praying church* and this is one of the secrets of their success. Ultimately, it is prayer and not programs which make a vibrant church. God wants us to be a praying church.

In verse 43 we see the result of all these things. "And fear came upon every soul; and many wonders and signs were done through the apostles." This church was a *powerful church*. Their commitment to God resulted in having a tremendous impact on their community. God wants His church to be powerful, to have an impact, to make a difference, to be the salt and light of the community. They were a powerful church.

Then in verses 44-45 we read, "And all who believed were together and they had all things in common and they sold their possession and goods and distributed them to all, as any had need." This church was a *servant church*. They believed in ministering to human needs, whether physical, emotional, or spiritual. Christ has called us to be servants, to be ministers. Too often our churches become self-serving. We forget that Jesus wants us to reach out to our community and meet the felt needs around us.

And the beautiful thing is that through service we find identity and meaning. Albert Schweitzer gave up everything in order to go to Africa and minister to the needs of people. Yet in that service he found the meaning of life. He once told a group of people, "I don't know what your destiny will be, but one thing I know; the only ones among you who will really be happy are those who will have sought and found how to serve."

Christ calls us to ministry—to reach out and care about the wounds and needs of others. This church was a servant church.

In verses 46 and 47 we read, "And day by day attending the temple together . . . praising God." This church was a *worshiping church*. Worship is central to the life of the church. I believe it is our first priority.

From worship we find the strength and motivation to witness and serve Christ in our daily lives.

Worship should be a vibrant and meaningful experience. Preparing and leading quality worship services is a priority for me as a pastor. Worship should be a priority for us all. This church was a worshiping church.

In the middle of verse 47 we read that the church was "having favor with all the people." They were also a *respected church*. These early Christians lived in such an exemplary way that they gained the respect of the community. God wants His church to be people of integrity.

And finally, the last words of the text say, "And the Lord added to their number day by day those who were being saved." We see lastly that they were a *growing church*. Every church has different potential for numerical growth, but most churches can and should grow. With commitment and concern, God's church can reach people for Christ and His church and grow.

Well, what a church! I hope you've caught a glimpse of what that early church looked like. They proclaimed the gospel, baptized new believers, taught God's word, and had a strong and loving fellowship. They were a church of prayer and had a powerful impact on their community. They were a servant church, they know how to worship, they were respected by their community, and they were growing.

And this church serves as our model. This is the kind of church God wants us to be. I know we don't always succeed. Neither did they. Sometimes we are a long way from the ideal and that discourages us. It reminds me of a favorite old story: A certain man woke to the sound of his alarm clock on Sunday morning. He turned it off and went back to sleep. His wife came in and said, "It's time to get up and get ready for church." He said, "I don't want to go to that church. It's full of hypocrites and they don't care one bit about me." He pulled up the covers and prepared to go back to sleep. But his wife insisted. "You have to get up and go to church," she said. He responded, "You give me one good reason why I should go." "I'll give you a reason" she said, "and a good one. You're the pastor of that church!"

Well, there are times when even pastors get discouraged about the church. I certainly do at times. But I'm committed to the church. For all its faults, the church is still God's vehicle for working in the world. I love the church. All that I am, I owe to God and to His church. And I've committed my life to working with the church, trying to help it become what God intends it to be.

And today, on Pentecost Sunday when we celebrate the birth of the church, it's good to look again and see what God wants of us. With the help of the Holy Spirit, we should strive to be like this church.

As I think about this early church and see it described, I have a prayer. It's a simple prayer: "Dear Lord, do it again, in our church. Amen."

Note

1. John Killinger, *Fundamentals of Preaching* (Philadelphia: Fortress Press, 1985), 13.

5

Christmas

When I served as a pastor, Christmas was my favorite time of the year. We decorated our sanctuary and celebrated the meaning of Christmas throughout December. The lighting of the Advent candles, the singing of Christmas music, the beauty of the poinsettias, handbells, and children's choirs, the retelling of the Christmas story—all joined together for a special season of worship.

My first book, *Getting Ready for Sunday: A Practical Guide for Worship Planning* (Broadman Press, 1989), has several worship ideas for observing the Christmas season. See pages 48-49, 136-137, and 165-175 for specific ideas.

Numerous worship and preaching resources are now available for observing Advent and Christmas. It's beyond the scope of this chapter to overview the meaning and observance of Advent. You can find such information in other resources. I will, however, share an order of worship and a sermon series called "The Manger People" which could be used during the Christmas season.

The Worship of God

They Came to Worship Him

Wise men from the East came to Jerusalem, saying, "Where is he who has been born king of the Jews? For we have seen his star in the East, and have come to worship him" (Matt. 1:1-2).

Prelude

Call to Worship . . . . Joy to the World . . . . Handbell Choir

The Greeting
Doxology
Hymn . . . . O Come, All Ye Faithful . . . . No. 81
The Lighting of the Advent Candles
Invocation

They Presented Him Gifts

Then, opening their treasures, they offered him gifts, gold, and frankincense, and myrrh (v. 11).
Special Music . . . . Children's Choir
Hymn . . . . O Little Town of Bethlehem . . . . No. 85
Offertory Prayer
Offering

They Fell Down and Worshiped Him

They rejoiced exceedingly with great joy; and going into the house they saw the child with Mary his mother, and they fell down and worshiped him (vv. 10-11).
Hymn . . . . Angels, from the Realms of Glory . . . . No. 87
Scripture Reading . . . . Matthew 2:1-12
Men's Quartet . . . . We Three Kings
Sermon . . . . Wise Worship from Wise Men

They Went Home Another Way

And being warned in a dream not to return to Herod, they departed to their own country by another way (v. 12).
Invitation Hymn . . . . Angels We Have Heard on High . . . . . No. 95
Benediction . . . . Go, Tell It on the Mountain . . . . . . Adult Choir
Postlude . . . . . . Good Christian Men, Rejoice . . . . . . Handbell Choir

Preaching Ideas

What follows is a series of sermons called "The Manger People." They could be used as individual sermons or as a series during the Christmas season.

The Manger People: Mary and Joseph
Matthew 1:18-25

Wayne Price tells the following Christmas story. One year his children received a set of tiny Nativity figures. When Christmas was over, the children refused to let them be packed away with the other Christmas things. They kept them in a cigar box on a shelf with their other toys. Periodically, throughout the year, one of them would get the box from the shelf and say, "Daddy, tell us the story about the manger people."[1]

During this Christmas season, we're going to turn our attention to these characters of the Nativity. The characters that surround the birth of Christ will help us capture the meaning and spirit of Christmas.

It's been over two thousand years since the manger people were involved in the events of the Nativity. However, they still beckon people to come to Bethlehem. They still capture the heart and imagination of millions.

There's a little town in Kentucky named Bethlehem. People from miles away come every year to the post office to have their Christmas cards postmarked "Bethlehem." But the community takes the season one step further. Every year they stage a live, outdoor Nativity scene. Most Kentucky Decembers are cold, windy, and wet. The townspeople are faithful, nevertheless. And so are hundreds of visitors. None of the characters speak, the only sound is recorded carols. And yet, people come to this out-of-the-way village by the carload. The people get out of their cars, stand in silence, and then drive away. Why do they come? Does it change them in some way? Regardless, they keep coming, year after year.[2]

The manger people are special people indeed. And today as I begin this series on the characters of the Nativity, I call your attention to two of the main characters, Mary and Joseph.

Mary and Joseph symbolize the essence of Christmas. If you'll study today's text and the other passages concerning their experience on that first Christmas, you'll see that Mary and Joseph represent Christmas as both a problem and a promise.

Christmas as a Problem

First, let's talk about Mary and Joseph and the first Christmas as a problem. Leave it to Charlie Brown and the Peanuts family of cartoon characters to explain Christmas in this way. In their annual television special, Charlie Brown just can't get into the Christmas spirit. Thus his little friend Linus observes: "Charlie Brown, you're the only person I know who can take a wonderful season like Christmas and turn it into a problem!"

But Christmas has been a problem from the very beginning. Mary and Joseph teach us that clearly. We forget about Mary's questions and fears when she discovered she was going to have a child. We don't think about the birth pains and weariness of that first night. Mary and Joseph, like all young parents, struggled with the hard task of caring for an infant. We forget that Mary and Joseph were real live people—struggling parents in a hard world of power politics and commerce. Christmas was a problem for Mary and Joseph.

Christmas began with an embarrassment. When Mary was found to be with child, Joseph wanted to "divorce her quietly" (Matt. 1:19). Christmas began as a scandal. And that was just the beginning of their problems.

Mary and Joseph were young newlyweds, poor, and expecting a child. They were forced to make a long hard journey to Bethlehem because a greedy foreign emperor wanted to squeeze even more tax dollars from the already poor people. Circumstances forced them to make a journey they should not have taken considering Mary's condition, and pay taxes they could not afford. Finally, when they arrived at Bethlehem, they looked frantically for a room, but could not find one. They were given a stable intended for housing animals, not people, to give birth to their child. The baby's bed was not the safe crib of home or hospital, but a feed trough. Then the baby was born, and for a moment they knew joy and celebration. But they soon learned that Herod wanted to kill their baby. Can you imagine? So they fled in horror, went to a strange country, and became refugees in a foreign land. And if you read on, the story gets even worse. We learn that Herod, mad as he was, killed all the infants in Beth-lehem in an attempt to murder Jesus.

The first Christmas was a problem. And the fact is, Christmas is still a problem for lots of people today. We are not all that different than Mary and Joseph. We too are struggling in a hard world. Like them, we are not in control of everything. Like them, we sometimes feel helpless, stepped on by powerful Caesars, and pushed around by unjust Herods. Perhaps our problem is physical illness, or loneliness, or financial worries. Maybe we're having family problems or maybe this is the first year we won't celebrate Christmas with our husband or wife.

Problems—Mary and Joseph had them, and so do we. And so does our world. Wars, violence, corruption, nuclear weapons, and hunger. Christmas then, is often a problem.

Christmas as a Promise

But if you read the story carefully, you'll see that Christmas is also a promise. In spite of all the difficulties, Mary and Joseph heard the good news of Christmas. "For that which is conceived in her is of the Holy Spirit; she will bear a son, and you shall call his name Jesus, for he will save his people from their sins. '. . . and his name shall be called Emman-uel' (which means, God with us)" (vv. 20-23).

So Christmas isn't just a problem, not just bad news. It holds great promise. It says God has broken into His world to save it and make it well. It says we can be forgiven and made new. It says that God, the God of all creation, is with us. Christmas is a great promise. It promises hope and meaning for a world full of problems.

In the year 1665 a great plague hit England. It wiped out many of the people. One year later, in 1666, a fire destroyed four-fifths of London. Samuel Pepys, writing in his diary, said: "All around me is death and despair. I don't think we can recover from this double tragedy." The bishop of London then was a man named Thomas Ken and he believed that they could come through that tragedy. He worked hard keeping faith and hope alive, sacrificing his life to minister to the needs of others. During those times he wrote a hymn, a song that you and I know so well, "Praise God, from Whom All Blessings Flow." In the midst of some of the darkest times in the history of England, in the midst of all that death and despair, came the cry, "Praise God, from whom all blessings flow."[3]

That's the message of Christmas. It says that in the midst of darkness and problems there is hope, there is promise. Mary and Joseph knew serious problems, just like each of us do. And yet they knew hope and joy and the presence of God. They knew that Jesus represented the hope of humanity, that he was indeed "God with us." Christmas is a promise, the greatest promise of all.

This dynamic that we see in Mary and Joseph, that of problem and promise, gets to the heart of Christmas. But more than that, it gets to the heart of the gospel. The gospel has a cross in its center. It has pain and death and problems. And we know of pain and problems. Life is full of the cross, of pain, struggle, fear, and hurt. Yet the gospel also has a resurrection, a promise that overcomes even death itself.

Most of us have heard of the great musician, George Frederick Handel. Late in his life things turned sour for Handel. The great composer lost his fortune, his health, and nearly all hope. Critics claimed that Handel was burned-out, old, and outdated—a "has-been." He was threatened with debtors' prison and was about out of hope. About that time Charles Jennens, a wealthy friend and writer, asked Handel to compose music and orchestration for a musical score on the biblical theme of redemption. The text was completely Scripture. And Handel, old and worn as he was, mustered enough grace to write the oratorio, *Messiah*. He thought it would take a year to write but he became inspired. He worked day and night and completed the project, all 260 pages of manuscript, in only twenty-four days. He fought back from failure to make his greatest contribution to the world's music. To one without a song, God's good news of redemption gave Handel the inspiration to write *Messiah*.[4]

When there is no song, or when there are problems—God comes again with new hope, new promise, a new song. Such is the story of Mary and Joseph and the first Christmas, a story about problems and yet about a promise, the greatest promise of all, the coming of Emmanuel—God with us.

The Manger People: The Shepherds
Luke 2:8-20

As I thought about the characters of the nativity, or "The Manger People" as we've been calling them, I remembered an old story.

It took place during art class in an elementary school. The teacher gave the children paper and crayons and told them to draw pictures on the theme of Christmas. The teacher noticed that one little boy drew an airplane. On the plane were three small figures. The teacher asked about the picture and its relation to Christmas. The boy explained that the three people were Mary, Joseph, and Jesus. "But what about the airplane?" asked the teacher, "what does that have to do with Christmas?" The boy said, "They are on the flight to Egypt." The teacher then noticed another figure in the cockpit. The teacher asked, "Who is that?" The boy replied, "Pontious the pilot."

As I continue this series on the manger people, I want to focus your attention on the shepherds, the first to hear the good news of Christmas. God's angels performed heaven's finest performance for these simple, ordinary, hardworking folk. And that is significant. Christmas must be for common folk if it is to mean anything at all. Because, if we're honest, all of us here today are just simple folk.

Although people are hung up on titles, status, popularity, and wealth—God is not. When He announced the news of Christ's birth He did so to shepherds. Christmas is for regular people: housewives, factory workers, postal employees, farmers, city workers, schoolteachers, retired folk, preachers . . . all of us who are here today. Christmas must say something to people like the shepherds or else it isn't worth all the fuss. But Christmas does have a word for the shepherds, and it has a word for us. Let's go once again to the manger people, and see the events that surround the shepherds.

The story begins this way (read v. 8). The story begins in the regular workaday world of shepherds. It starts in the routine, the typical, the ordinary.

But all of a sudden, God breaks into the ordinary. He confronts these simple shepherds in a remarkable way (read v. 9). As we follow the story

I'd like you to note three things about their experience. The shepherds heard the good news, they saw the good news, and they shared the good news.

They Heard the Good News

The story continues in verse 10 (read vv. 10-14).

It came time for the annual Christmas play. Sarah was given the part of the angel. She practiced her line faithfully, "Behold, I bring you good tidings of great joy." Over and over again she practiced it, "Behold I bring you good tidings of great joy." The night of the play finally arrived. Sarah walked on stage but could not remember her line. Dead silence followed. Finally, she blurted out, "Boy, do I have good news for you!"

The shepherds heard the good news. And they needed some good news. They had more than their share of bad news. Every time they turned around they got word about a heavier tax levy or stricter regulations from the Romans or their own religious leaders. Their sheep often died or were injured, bad weather often hurt the grazing land, and it got lonely away from family and friends. They needed some good news.

And so do we. We get bad news all the time. We've had more than our fair share of it this year. We, like the shepherds, need some good news.

And they heard good news. News about a savior. For all our modern sophistication, we still need a Savior. We are still plagued by guilt and low self-esteem, we desperately need to be forgiven and made whole, and only a savior can do that. They heard good news about a Christ, a deliverer. And we need a deliverer today, someone to deliver us from meaninglessness, from the trivial pursuit of materialism, from hopelessness. And they heard good news about a Lord. A Lord who would give people purpose and direction. A Lord who we can follow and serve, who will point the way for living. And they heard good news about peace on earth. Peace—it seems elusive doesn't it? We live in a world of war and violence. And as long as men choose the way of pride and selfishness, war will continue. But the good news is that peace is available. We can know the "peace of God which passes all understanding" (Phil. 4:7). In our world of anxiety and tranquilizers, peace can be found. For this Savior, this Christ—can offer peace in our hearts. We can know Him, the Emmanuel, God with us, and we can find peace.

They Saw the Good News

Let's read on in the story. In verse 15 we read these words (read vv. 15-16).

They didn't just hear, they saw. They went to Bethlehem and saw this baby. And seeing is important. It's like the nurse on the television program a few years ago.

She was bitter, tired, and resentful. Her husband had left her with four mouths to feed—three besides her own: twin girls about twelve, and a bright, aggressive boy—sixteen going on thirty. It was almost Christmas and she was working a lot of overtime, partly because she was needed at the hospital and partly because she wanted the extra money to buy presents. She had the flu at Thanksgiving but hadn't taken time to go to bed so now she was more tired and run-down than usual. Everything seemed to be going wrong—life was coming apart at the seams. Her father, who lived in a rest home, fell and broke his hip, and wrote her to come and see him. She wanted to go but didn't have the time or money to make the trip. Her girls wanted those cute adoptable dolls for Christmas. She saved and bought them, but was worried because she didn't have much left to buy a nice gift for her son. Then one evening she discovered some drugs in her son's schoolbook, and they had a great fight about that. She was awake most of the night, crying, angry, and unhappy. The next day was one of those impossible days at the hospital, days you want to forget . . . blowups with a couple of irritable patients, a run-in with a floor nurse, a charming old lady dying in an operation, a collision with an orderly that sent a meal tray crashing to the floor. Nothing went right. "Life," she said, "is hell."

On her way home, wondering how she would manage with her son, she heard the sound of carols coming from an old brownstone church. She almost passed the church, then stopped, turned around, and went in, as if some power beyond herself were drawing her. She sat on the back pew. Some children in bathrobes were staging the Nativity scene. The baby in Mary's arms was not a doll but a real baby. She saw it raise its hand and try to grab the girl's nose. After another reading and another hymn, the baby became restless and began to cry. The girl cradled it, tried to soothe it, but it squalled. The little boy standing at the pulpit could not be heard reading his part. Finally a woman came up onto the stage and took the baby from the girl to quiet it. The nurse assumed it was the baby's mother. The baby still would not be consoled, and the woman carried it out of the chancel and through a door at the side. The little congregation was singing "Silent Night."

Something lit up the nurse's eyes and she smiled. Her face became youthful and animated again. *It was a real baby*, she thought. *A real baby! Jesus was a real baby. It wasn't just a story. He was real. He cried. He wet. He caused His mother anguish. God really cares about real life!*

As she slipped out of the church into the night air, buttoning her coat, there was a radiance about her face. She smiled at people in the street. She stopped for groceries and bought some peppermint ice cream for dessert. When she entered the apartment she transformed it. It was as if the whole place became suddenly bright and happy. The world was a different place because she had seen the baby in the manger. The baby who makes everything different—even history itself. And that night she was like a child again, bringing laughter and joy into her home. The child in her had seen the eternal Child in the manger, and it changed her life.[5]

They Shared the Good News

These shepherds heard the good news and they saw the good news. But that's not the end of the story. They also shared the good news (read vv. 17-18).

After the Christmas holidays, we often feel let down. The kids get bored with their toys and we have to go back to our regular life. But these shepherds felt no letdown. For them, Christmas had just begun. They went about telling everyone the good news. And what good news! News about a Savior, a Christ, a Lord, and about peace on earth.

And God says to us, His church, "Tell the good news!" We are not supposed to keep the good news of Christmas a secret. Others desperately need to know. Those who live in our neighborhood, who work with us, who go to our school—people in our community need to know. Share with them what Christ means to you. Bring them to this place so they can hear and see the good news proclaimed.

God needs laypeople, people like these shepherds, to tell the good news. The text says that people marveled at the shepherds. People expect to hear religion from professional religious folks like myself, but they are intrigued and impressed when regular folks tell them about Christ. The shepherds shared the good news. God tells us to do the same thing.

That wraps up the story of these simple shepherds. They heard the good news, they saw the good news, and they shared the good news.

The story concludes like it began. Back in the regular workaday world, back in the routine. We read about that in verse 20 (read). They went back, but there was a major difference. They now had a song to sing and a story to tell.

The Manger People: The Christ Child
John 1:1-14; Matthew 1:21-23

Last week, my wife and I went to a Christmas production at another church. As we entered, I admired the Nativity scene in the vestibule. Upon closer examination, however, I noticed that Jesus was missing. The shepherds, the wise men, Mary and Joseph—they were all there. But somebody had stolen the baby Jesus.

As I thought about that Nativity scene, it seemed to represent what often happens at Christmas. We have all the trappings of Christmas—music, parties, gifts, and trees—but sometimes we leave out Jesus. It's as if somebody took the Christ child and left us with everything else.

We can have all the Christmas externals—the songs, gifts, and decorations—but unless we have Jesus, we've missed the point. We can even look at the manger people—Mary and Joseph, the shepherds, and the wise men—but unless we focus on the Christ child, we've missed the meaning of Christmas.

So let's go again to Bethlehem, to the manger people, and take a close look at the baby in the manger.

It's amazing to consider the birth of Jesus. God decided to enter our world in a personal way, to save the world from its sin. But He entered our world as a tiny and vulnerable baby, and a poor one at that. This baby didn't even have a room in the inn, but was born in a stable with a feed trough as His bed. Yet this baby was the most significant child ever born. Through this child, God is revealed. And through this child, humanity is redeemed.

Through This Child, God Is Revealed

In Christ, "The Word became flesh and dwelt among us" (John 1:14). God made Himself fully known in Jesus. As Hebrews 1:3 says, "He reflects the glory of God and bears the very stamp of his nature." God had made Himself known in many ways through the centuries, but in this child, God fully revealed Himself.

In a famous cathedral in Rome, a magnificent painting radiates beauty. Every colorful detail has been painted with patience. But for centuries, few visitors to the cathedral actually appreciated this work of art. The problem was its location. It was at the top of the cathedral, on the dome. People who tried to look at it received a stiff neck and eyestrain. This physical discomfort prevented enjoyment and appreciation of the masterpiece.

Finally, somebody with common sense solved the centuries-old problem. A large mirror was placed just above the floor level. A sight once too distant and difficult to behold was in effect, brought down to a more human level. Guests can now be seated, study, and appreciate all the splendor of this superb painting.[6]

In a way, this is the story of the Christ child. God, once seen only partially, can now be seen clearly in Jesus. Jesus reveals God, shows God's nature, tells us God's teachings. In Christ, God is revealed."The Word became flesh and dwelt among us."

Through this child, humanity is redeemed.—In our second text this morning we read that the Christ child will "Save his people from their sins"(Matt.1:21). This is the most important news of Christmas. Through Christ, we can be made whole and new, we can be saved.

Christ came, lived among us, and suffered for us. Because of Him, we can be forgiven. Through Him we can know God's presence in our life in a real and personal way. Through Christ, we are reconciled with God. This is the great news of Christmas.

This child in the manger represents a miracle. In Jesus, God revealed Himself to the world. He is the clearest picture of God that we can have. And in Jesus, humanity is redeemed. Through Him we are made whole, we are forgiven, and cleansed. Through Him we become God's children. God revealed, humanity redeemed—such is the miracle of this newborn child in Bethlehem.

Through This Child, Miracles Still Happen

Some time ago, I heard Wayne Dehoney tell a story which illustrates how Christmas continues to be a miracle even today. It is a beautiful, incredible story. It's almost unbelievable but it is true. It comes from the experience of Reverend H. C. Shade when he pastored the First Reformed Church of Nyack, New York.

Reverend Shade and his wife were sent by their denomination to a shabby, little church to help revive it. The people had become careless and indifferent and the church was in bad repair. They poured their lives into the church. They visited the membership and slowly, but surely, the church began to show new signs of life. They worked hard to refurbish and redecorate the church as they came to their first Christmas Eve service. They were excited and pleased with how well the church had done. They had an acceptable church building now and a good congregation to celebrate Christmas.

Just before Christmas a terrible storm came and tore off part of the roof. The rains soaked the furnishings and a great mass of plaster fell from the wall behind the pulpit and left a great gaping hole. As they cleaned up the mess, this pastor and his wife wept. What could they do? They could dry things off and pick up the plaster, but the hole behind the pulpit—well, nothing could be done.

That evening they went to a youth benefit auction. The auctioneer held up an old tablecloth—at least fifteen feet long, but no one was interested in this obsolete piece of linen, although it was beautifully embroidered. Reverend Shade's eyes met his wife's eyes. They both had the same idea. They bought it for $6.50. When they went to the church and stretched the tablecloth out it fit perfectly over the gaping hole. God had provided a beautiful tapestry, and as the lights played on the embroidery work it looked as though it was made just exactly for that place. That was God's miracle for them that Christmas.

But God was not through. On Christmas Eve, the pastor saw an elderly lady standing at the bus stop near the church. In broken English she asked, "What time is the next bus?" "The bus comes just once an hour and you have just missed one," explained the pastor. He invited her to come inside for it was bitterly cold. She explained, "I live in another community some distance away. Someone had advertised for a housekeeper and guardian for a child, so I came in answer to the ad. But my English was not good enough. Maybe I was too old."

They went inside, and as she walked to the front of the church, she looked up and saw that beautiful tablecloth. Her eyes lit up, she smiled, and the pastor explained about the hole. She walked closer and said, I can't believe it! Where did you get this?" And he told her. She said, "You will not believe this, but this is my tablecloth! I would recognize it anywhere. I can tell and show you all about it." She then explained every detail of the embroidery.

She continued her story, "My husband gave this to me when we were in Vienna before the days of Hitler. He gave it to me one Christmas." The pastor asked, "Where is your husband now?" "Oh, he is dead. When Hitler came into Austria we had to flee. He sent me to Switzerland and he was to follow but did not, and I never heard from him. He did not make it and the word I have is that he died in a concentration camp. That is my tablecloth, however." The pastor offered to give it back to her. "No, no, let God have it." And she went on to her bus.

That evening, Christmas Eve, the congregation gathered along with many visitors from town. Among the group was the old Austrian clock maker and repairman. When he saw the cloth he said, "That tablecloth is exactly like one my wife had in the old country."

With that the wheels began to spin. *Could it be?* the pastor thought. He went home, pulled out his newspaper, and found the ad where somebody in the community advertised for a housekeeper and guardian of a child. He went to that house and asked, "Did a woman with a German accent come here today to interview?" "Yes." "Do you have her name and address?" "Yes." Taking that information he went to the household of that woman and brought her back to town. He then brought the Austrian man to meet her. He was her husband, and they were reunited on that Christmas Eve. Reverend Shade said, "Once again, God worked a miracle at Christmas, as he worked it two thousand years ago."

This story reminds me that the miracle of Christmas continues even today. When God, through Jesus Christ, comes into our hearts, miracles are performed. Lives are changed and dreams become realities, hope becomes brightened and joy becomes full.

What of this child in the manger? He is the Christ, the Son of the living God. He came to reveal God. He came to redeem humanity. And through Him, miracles still occur.

The Manger People: The Wise Men
Matthew 2:1-12

Today we make our final visit to the "Manger People." We've looked at Mary and Joseph, the shepherds, and the Christ child. Today we'll look at the wise men.

When I was a child, my friends and I used to sing "We Three Kings Of Orient Are." Boys will be boys, however, and we changed up the words a bit. We sang, "We three kings of Orient are, tried to smoke a rubber cigar, it was loaded and exploded, now we no longer are." The song continued, "We two kings of Orient are, tried to smoke a rubber cigar, it was loaded and exploded, now we no longer are." The final verse went like this, "Me the king of Orient are, tried to smoke a rubber cigar, it was loaded and exploded, now we no longer are." Upon finishing the song we immediately sang, "God Rest Ye Merry, Gentlemen!"

Well, just who were these wise men? We know very little about them other than a few verses of Scripture in Matthew 2. Legend has it that they were kings, but the Bible simply says they were wise men from the East. Legend not only says they were kings, but actually gave them names. There is even a cathedral in Germany which claims to have their remains buried there!

We don't know much about these wise men. But we do know that they came to worship Jesus. And in their worship, we can learn how to better worship. Let's look today at how these wise men worshiped Christ the Lord.

They Came to Worship

"Now when Jesus was born in Bethlehem, . . . behold, wise men from the East came to Jerusalem, saying, 'Where is he who has been born king of the Jews? For we have seen his star in the East, and have come to worship him' "(Matt.2:1-2). It all starts here, doesn't it? They came. Across a long distance, across alien territory, following a star of hope. They came, and that is significant. We can't worship if we don't come. Oh, I know people say that they can worship just as well on the lake or in the deer woods, but we know that just doesn't happen.

Worship begins when we come to church to worship God. And we need to come and do it together. Something special happens when we gather together to worship the Lord. Nothing else in the life of the church is more important.

I'll never forget an elderly woman in one of the churches I served as a pastor. One Sunday she said to me, "Brother Martin, I had a hard time getting to church today. I can barely walk to my Sunday School class anymore. But when I can't walk anymore, I'll crawl." She knew how important it was to come.

I know that our worship services aren't always wonderful. Sometimes they are dull or miss the mark. Yet worship is extremely important. It puts us in contact with God. It shapes our life. It's important to us, to God, and to our church. So the first thing to notice about these wise men is that they came.

They offered their praise.—The wise men came. Second, they offered praise to the newborn Christ. The text says, "and going into the house they saw the child with Mary his mother, and they fell down and worshiped him."

God is worthy of our worship. When we come to worship, we should be like these wise men. We should bow with awe and adoration and offer our praise to God.

When we worship, we encounter the living and holy God. Like Isaiah of old, we come to worship to see the Lord, high and lifted up. Our only response is to offer praise. We can do it through singing and prayer and many other ways, but if we are to truly worship, we, like the wise men, must offer up our praise.

They Offered Their Gifts

"Then, opening their treasures, they offered him gifts, gold and frankincense and myrrh" (v. 11). When people really worship, they offer tangible gifts to God. These wise men gave gifts, and they gave valuable gifts.

True worship involves gift giving. It is a natural response when we stand before God. In one of his sermons, John Killinger told his congregation a story about Robert E. Lee I'd like to share.

Several months after Robert E. Lee ceased to be the great general of the Confederacy, he was offered the presidency of Washington College in Lexington, Virginia. The school was bankrupt. Only forty students had been recruited for the coming fall. Lexington was a remote little village, accessible only by canal boat or by stagecoach over twisting, mountain roads. But Lee regarded the invitation to be president as a call of Providence, and he accepted. Soon after he moved to Lexington, important people from all over the country began making their way to Lexington to visit him. And before they left, they pressed gifts of money and property on him for the school. They couldn't help themselves. In the presence of his greatness, they felt the need to give something. And, under their giving, the school flourished.[7]

That's the way it is in worship. When we come into the presence of the greatness of God, we'll respond by giving gifts.

They Went Home a Different Way

They came, they offered praise, and they offered gifts. There's one more thing, however, that I want to point out. After they worshiped, "they departed to their own country by another way" (v. 12).

This verse, of course, clearly speaks about geography. They went home a different route than they came. But I think this is also true in a spiritual sense. After encountering Jesus, the wise men were different.

When we come to worship and offer our praise and gifts—when we encounter the living God—we will go home a different way. Our lives will be touched in some way by God, and we won't be exactly the same as we were before.

My sincere prayer is that God will help us to have the kind of worship experiences that would send us home a different way. And I believe that if we'll come faithfully, and offer up praise, and give our gifts—that's exactly what will happen to us.

Notes

1. *Proclaim,* October, November, December 1982, 8.
2. Ibid.
3. *Proclaim,* October, November, December 1986, 20.
4. C. W. Bess, *Sermons for the Seasons* (Nashville: Broadman Press, 1985), 31-32.
5. From a sermon by John Killinger, "What Do You See in Christmas?" December 15, 1985, First Presbyterian Church, Lynchburg, VA.
6. Bess, 15.
7. From a sermon by John Killinger, "A Pattern for Worship in the New Year," January 6, 1985, First Presbyterian Church, Lynchburg, VA.

Part II
Special Sundays from the Secular Calendar

6

Mother's Day

As with most secular holidays, I do not feel obligated to observe Mother's Day and Father's Day. They do, however, offer a good opportunity to affirm and encourage the Christian family. Therefore, when these two days arrive, I usually focus the worship service and sermon on the family.

Worship Ideas

When I served as a pastor, I usually based the worship service on Mother's Day around the hymn, "God Give Us Christian Homes." I used the same service, with a few adjustments, for Father's Day. I did not worry about repeating this worship outline year by year. Familiarity with the worship outline became a strength rather than a weakness. The service worked well for us and the congregation looked forward to these special days of worship. Although we used the same basic order of worship, we changed some of the details. The order of worship follows.

The Worship of God

God Give Us Christian Homes

Prelude
Call to Worship . . . . Youth Choir
The Greeting
Chorus . . . . The Bond of Love
Invocation
Hymn: God Give Us Christian Homes . . . . No. 397
Parent-Child Dedication

Homes Where the Mother, in Queenly Quest,
Strives to Show Others Thy Way Is Best

Recognition of Mothers
Scripture Reading .... Proverbs 31:10-11,25-29
Testimony

Homes Where the Bible Is Loved and Taught

Scripture Readings
Hymn .... Holy Bible, Book Divine .... No. 139
Offering

Homes Where the Master's Will Is Sought

Special Music.............................. Children's Choir
Sermon
Invitation Hymn ..... Have Thine Own Way, Lord ...... No. 349
Benediction
Postlude

Parent-Child Dedication

A Parent-Child dedication can add much to Mother's Day. Parents with young children need to be contacted several weeks before this service. Explain the purpose of the service and invite them to participate.

Begin the dedication by inviting those who are participating to come to the front of the sanctuary. A suggested ceremony follows. You may want to print it as a bulletin insert in your order of worship.

Introduction

We come now to a special service of dedication for these families and for us as a church family. The precedent for the ceremony of child dedication is found in Holy Scripture. In Deuteronomy 6:4-7 God tells us to teach His law diligently unto our children. In 1 Samuel 1:24-28 we find Hannah presenting Samuel to the Lord. In Luke 2:22-32 Mary and Joseph present Jesus to God at the temple. In Mark 10:13-16 we hear Jesus tell His disciples to allow the little children to come to Him. In

Ephesians 6:4 the apostle Paul told parents to bring up their children in the nurture and admonition of the Lord.

Charge to the Parents

Pastor: Parents, do you desire that your child grow in the nurture and admonition of the Lord?
Parents: We do.
Pastor: As parents, do you covenant with God and with the members of this church to assist your child in growing, as Jesus did, in wisdom and stature and in favor with God and man?
Parents: We do.
Pastor: Because you desire for your child a knowledge of the Scripture and a loving, obedient attitude toward God and His Son, Jesus Christ, do you promise to use your home and the church to accomplish this task?
Parents: We do.

Charge to the Congregation

Pastor: Recognizing the responsibility that you have as a congregation toward each of these children, do you agree to love and protect them, showing always a Christian spirit? Do you promise that by giving your time, talents, and money, you will do your part in providing Christian instruction and training? If you will accept this responsibility, say, we do.
Congregation: We do.

Presentation of Certificates

(You can purchase or order these from a Christian Book Store.)

Prayer of Dedication

Scripture readings—Consider inviting an entire family to read Scripture during this service. They could each read a passage which deals with the family, or they could divide up the verses from a single text. Numerous passages of Scripture would be appropriate. Consider, for example, the following: Deuteronomy 6:4-7; Ephesians 6:1-4; 1 Samuel 1:27-28; Proverbs 1:7-9; Psalm 127:3-5; Proverbs 31; and Mark 10:13-16.

Preaching Ideas

Preaching on Mother's Day can be a difficult assignment. The Bible is not full of texts which readily serve as a Mother's Day sermon.

One solution is to broaden your subject. Mother's Day sermons do not have to focus directly on mothering. Think in terms of the Christian family. You can preach sermons on parenting, marriage, and family life in general. I often preach a series of sermons on the Christian family during this time of the year. I've preached series such as "Principles of Parenting," "Principles of Partnership," and "The Christian Family." Any sermon dealing with the family is appropriate on Mother's Day. When I preached a series of sermons on the Ten Commandments I planned it so that I would preach on the Fifth Commandment—honoring your father and mother—on Mother's Day.

Of course, you don't have to preach on the family on Mother's Day. One year I preached a sermon on commitment to Christ. Although I mentioned the need for families to be committed to the Lord, it was not a family sermon. I did, however, take notice of the day. We focused on the Christian family through a special prayer for parents, a Scripture reading on the subject, and a testimony. If you focus at least some of the worship service on the family, your sermon does not have to relate directly to Mother's Day. If you are in the middle of a series, or you don't have any good sermon ideas on the subject, don't feel obligated to preach that direction. I would, however, at least refer to Mother's Day in prayers and other places in the service.

I don't have any original "sugar stick" sermons for Mother's Day. My best Mother's Day sermons come from series on the family, and space doesn't permit me to share another sermon series. I hope to write another book in the future concerning preaching on the family.

My best ideas for individual Mother's Day sermons came from other preachers. I'll share two sermon ideas, and then a complete sermon summary.

A few years ago, John Killinger preached a Mother's Day sermon called, "The Best Supporting Actress."[1] He began the sermon by talking about the Academy Awards. In all of our excitement about the best picture, best actress, and best actor, we don't pay much attention to the awards, "Best Supporting Actor" and "Best Supporting Actress." Killinger points out, however, that these people are extremely important. He says: "They are the mothers and fathers, the aunts and uncles, the older friends and co-conspirators, who enrich the stage around the stars and weave the fabric of make-believe with such consummate artistry that the stars are able to shine with beauty and lustre. They are indispensible to the theater. Without them, the stars themselves would be diminished."

Killinger says this same dynamic is also true in real life. Each of us is, in a sense, the star of the drama we are living. Around us are supporting actors and actresses—other persons who make our part richer and more meaningful. And perhaps the most significant supporting actresses are our mothers.

At this point, Killinger turns his attention to Mary, the mother of Jesus, whom he claims is Christ's best supporting actress. She was there in the beginning, even before Jesus was born, willing to be God's vessel (Luke 1:38). She carried this child to birth under difficult circumstances.

She was also there during the formative years, nurturing, loving, and teaching Him. Luke 2:41-52 illustrates the strong religious heritage Jesus gained from His early home life. The religious authorities were "amazed at his understanding and his answers" (v. 47). Mary certainly helped contribute to this spiritual maturity.

Mary's support, however, didn't stop there. She was always available for Christ, even when He was a grown man (see Mark 3, for example). And Mary was there in the end. When all the disciples fled, Mary was at the cross, watching her beloved son die (see John 19).

When you examine the evidence, Mary was indeed Jesus' "Best Supporting Actress." She serves as a role model for all mothers. And on Mother's Day, we celebrate the thousands of mothers who serve in this capacity. We thank God for their support in our lives.

I took Killinger's idea and developed my own sermon which was well received in my congregation. Perhaps you can do the same.

Years ago, Wayne Dehoney preached a sermon called, "Our Other

Mothers." I did not hear the sermon nor even read it. I simply saw the title and text. It intrigued me, however, and I hope to develop such a sermon in the future.

The text is Exodus 2:1-10. This story tells how the daughter of Pharaoh found Moses in the river, and how she took him home and raised him. She was not his real mother, but she nurtured him and invested her life into caring for him.

Our churches have many women who are not mothers. Many wanted to be, but could not. But many of these women still invest their love and life into children. Perhaps they work in the church nursery or teach a children's Sunday School class. Perhaps they are a schoolteacher or a kind neighbor to the neighborhood children. Perhaps they are a favorite aunt. These are our "other mothers" and they are extremely important. Mother's Day would be a wonderful time to affirm these women. You could illustrate the sermon by telling of one such "other mother" in your life or the lives of your children. This idea has great potential. Perhaps you can make something of this idea and preach "Our Other Mothers" for this year's Mother's Day sermon.

As you may know, I now serve as editor of *Proclaim* magazine. *Proclaim* helps thousands of pastors and music ministers with their preaching and worship ministry. Every issue is chock-full of usable worship and preaching ideas. Of course, I highly recommend the magazine! A few years ago, I was looking for an idea for Mother's Day. I looked back at old issues of *Proclaim* and found an excellent sermon. The April, May, June 1983 edition has a sermon by Brian Harbour called, "A Mother Who Passed on Her Faith." I'm including it here. Perhaps you used it in 1983. If so, enough time has passed to use it again.

A Mother Who Passed on Her Faith
2 Timothy 1:5

Some time back I saw an interesting contrast made between two men who lived in Northampton, Massachusetts, in the early seventeen hundreds. One was a preacher named Jonathan Edwards. The other was an unbeliever named Max Jukes.

Jonathan Edwards married a devout Christian girl and from their union came 729 descendants. Of these, 300 were ministers, sixty-five were university presidents, sixty were authors of good books, three were U.S. congressmen, and one was vice-president of the United States. Most made a significant contribution to society.

Max Jukes, who lived not far from Jonathan Edwards, was an unbeliever who married an unbeliever; and from their union came 1,026 descendants. Of these, 300 died early in life, 100 went to prison for an average of thirteen years, 200 were prostitutes, 100 were alcoholics. The descendants of this man cost the state over a million dollars to care for them.

What does determine how a child will turn out? What is the primary force which molds the life of an individual and determines what he will accomplish in life?

The answer is obviously not geographic location, for productive people and parasites of society both come from all places.

Educational opportunities are not the answer. There are enough Ph.D's in prison to staff any college. Neither is denominational affiliation the key. When Billy Graham preached once at a prison, the warden leaned over and said, "It might comfort you to know that 50 percent of our inmates are Baptists!" Some comfort!

Sheer talent is not the secret. There are talented crooks as well as talented saints.

Even circumstances do not seem to be the key factor, for some of life's most productive citizens have come out of the most unpleasant circumstances.

What does determine what a child will become? I believe the answer is: parents. I remember seeing a cartoon of a kangaroo with a baby kangaroo peeping out of the pouch. This caption was at the bottom: "His mother determines his point of view." It's true.

Because that truth relates to our responsibilities as parents today and is applicable to how our children will turn out, I think it would be instructive for us to look at a biblical mother who passed on her faith to her son and see how she did it. Eunice was her name, and she is mentioned in only one verse in the New Testament. Yet that one brief reference has exalted her to a place of preeminence. For what is she exalted? Did she start a church? Was she a great missionary? Was she an outstanding author? a successful Christian businesswoman? No, she became a heroine of the Bible and was honored as one of God's dear saints because she passed on her faith to her son.

How did she do it? What were the practices that enabled Eunice to pass on her faith to her son?

She Planted It

The first obvious factor in the story of Eunice and her son, Timothy, is that she planted the faith in his life at an early age. From the first day of his life, he had a constant reminder of the importance of faith and that reminder was his name. She named him Timothy which meant, "God-fearing."

Eunice could not put the fruit of faith in her son's life. She knew that. But she could plant the seeds which she hoped someday would blossom into faith. She could not make her son fear God, but she could give him that name to live up to. The process of passing on her faith to her son began the day he was born.

We parents, in every area of life, want what is best for our children. So we try to determine what is best, and then we go about planting the ideas and developing the personal habits that will enable our children to realize the best, to experience fulfillment. If we do that with personal behavior, education, diet, and grooming, why shouldn't we do it for spiritual things?

When you do not plant the seeds of faith in the life of your child, when you don't create a kind of spiritual climate in your home that will influence your child in matters of religion, you are not being tolerant. You are negligent.

Eunice was able to pass on her faith to her son because she started the day he was born by planting the seeds of faith in his life.

She Taught It

Notice a second factor. Not only did Eunice plant the faith in Timothy's life at the beginning but she also taught him the faith as he grew up.

We see this not in our text but in 2 Timothy 3:14-15 where Paul wrote "You, however, continue in the things you have learned and become convinced of, knowing from whom you have learned them; and that from childhood you have known the sacred writings which are able to give you the wisdom that leads to salvation through faith which is in Christ Jesus" (NASB).

Can that be said about our sons and daughters that from childhood they have known the Bible and what it says?

If our children are to learn to love God, we have to teach them. If they are to become men and women of faith, we have to guide them. If they are to know from childhood the sacred Scriptures, it will be because we have committed ourselves to teaching the Bible in the home.

To pass on our faith to our children we must teach them the faith as revealed in the Word of God in our home. That was the secret of Eunice's success.

She Lived It

Eunice planted the faith in Timothy's life. Then she taught the faith to him. And finally, she lived it.

Paul spoke in our text of the "unfeigned"(KJV) faith of Eunice and her mother. The *New American Standard Bible* uses the word "sincere." *Phillips* has "genuine faith." The Greek word derives from a verb from which we get our word *hypocrite*. A hypocrite was one who acted beneath a guise, an actor behind a mask. But Paul said Eunice's faith was unhypocritical. It was not a put-on faith. It was real. The faith Eunice claimed to have publicly she also lived privately. She lived her faith at home.

Josh Billings, the American humorist, gave some good advice when he said, "Train up a child in the way he should go, and walk there yourself once in a while." That's good advice, because the single most powerful impact you have on your children is not what you say but what you do, not the convictions you claim to have but the convictions you really have as evidenced by the way you live your life.

Is this the best of times or the worst of times for the family? Today can be the best, if we will be faithful in focusing on the God-ordained functions of the family.

Note

1. John Killinger, "The Best Supporting Actress," May 12, 1985, First Presbyterian Church, Lynchburg, VA.

7

Memorial Day

Since Memorial Day is a time to remember loved ones who have died, it offers a good opportunity for the church to deal with the subject of grief. The service and sermon on Memorial Day weekend can offer encouragement, comfort, and hope to those who grieve. Since grief is such a natural part of life, it is appropriate that this subject be dealt with in worship.

The Worship of God

"For They Shall Be Comforted"

Comfort Through Praise

Prelude
Responsive Reading.................................... No. 522
Hymn .... O Worship the King .... No. 30
The Greeting
Doxology
Invocation

Comfort Through Praise

Discipline of Silence
Pastoral Prayer
The Lord's Prayer

Comfort Through Testimony

Hymn . . . . When We All Get to Heaven. . . . . No. 491
Testimony. . . . . God's Grace for My Grief
Hymn . . . . Great Is Thy Faithfulness . . . . No. 216
Offering

Comfort Through Proclamation

Old Testament Reading. . . . . Psalm 23
New Testament Reading. . . . . John 11:17-27
Anthem. . . . . Choir
Sermon . . . . Good Grief. . . . . Pastor
Hymn . . . . I Know that My Redeemer Liveth . . . . No. 122
Benediction
Postlude

Good Grief
Matthew 5:4

A boy was deeply in love with a girl in his eighth-grade class. He finally got enough nerve to ask her out for a date—his first ever. He was nervous and asked his friend for advice. "You are experienced at this," he said, "what should I do?" His friend said, "Girls love flowers; take her flowers."

Well, the big night came. The boy went to her front door with a dozen roses. When he handed her the flowers she immediately hugged and kissed him. He started to run away. "Wait a minute" she shouted, "I didn't mean to scare you." "I'm not scared" he said. "Then why are you running away?" she asked. "To buy some more flowers!" he said.

As the saying goes, "Ain't love grand." And yes, love is grand. Love between couples, love for children, love between friends, love in the church family. Love is grand.

But love has a cost. For when we lose someone we love, it hurts. Tomorrow is Memorial Day—a day to remember those whom we've loved and lost. Flowers will be left at thousands of graves throughout our country and a lot of grief will be experienced.

Grief comes from any significant loss. People grieve when they lose a job or business, when their children move away, when their friend is transferred. Grief comes when dreams die or families fail. Any significant loss brings an element of grief.

And so on this Memorial weekend it is appropriate to speak of grief. And I'm going to focus on ultimate grief—grief over the death of a loved one. My text today comes from Jesus' Sermon on the Mount—one of the Beatitudes. The passage, Matthew 5:4 says, "Blessed are those who mourn, for they shall be comforted." I'd like you to repeat that verse with me this morning (ask entire congregation to repeat the verse).

In this short passage of Scripture three key words stand out: (1) *mourn*, (2) *blessed*, and (3) *comforted*. I'd like to hang my sermon on those words today and try to discover how God can help us experience good grief.

Mourn

In this passage, Jesus speaks about mourning. Mourning is a common biblical term. It means to lament, to grieve. But many of us are uncomfortable with grief. We don't quite know how to handle it.

A minister tells about a funeral service he performed. An old woman was crying at the top of her voice moments before the service began. "Why? Why did this have to happen? He was so good!" And a forty-three-year-old man wearing a three-piece suit became very uncomfortable and said, "Can't anybody make her shut up? Can't somebody give her a sedative?" The fact is, said the minister, that the old woman was the only one in the room who was in her right mind. It was appropriate to grieve over her great loss.[1]

Grief is often spoken of in the Bible. It is a natural experience. Read David's lament over the deaths of Saul and Jonathan, or Abraham's mourning over the death of Sarah. In Bible days the people had rituals of grieving which helped them express their grief in healthy ways.

Grief is the natural expression of loss. It is as natural as eating when you are hungry or sleeping when you are tired. Our faith does not protect us from feeling grief. It always bothers me to go to a funeral and be told that I should not be sad or grieve. I can relate to the seminary professor who attended his mother's funeral. Well-meaning Christian friends said to this professor, who was obviously grieving, "Don't feel bad. Don't cry. Isn't it wonderful that she's gone to be with the Lord?" He smiled weakly, he said, and gave a token nod of assent to his friends' comments. Inside, however, he felt ready to explode with anger, grief, and frustration. He wanted to shout at the top of his lungs, "No, it's not wonderful that she's gone! I miss her and I hurt and I'm going to cry as much as I want."[2]

We cannot avoid grief. We can, however, learn more about it. In that way we will be better equipped to deal with it.

Some fairly predictable stages are experienced by most people when they face grief. To be sure, the stages are not clear-cut, they don't move in a straight and simple line. But there is a fairly predictable pattern. Wayne Oates, a well-known pastoral counselor, points out six stages which most grieving people experience.[3]

1. A time of shock when we first get the news.

2. A stage of numbness as we try to absorb the shock. This is a God-given numbness—it protects us from the full blow all at once, and it helps us get through the demands of funeral preparations and those first few horrible days.

3. The stage of mixed belief and disbelief. You know your loved one is dead but there are moments when it's like they are still alive. During this stage it is common to dream they are alive—then to wake up and know they are not.

4. The stage when we accept the reality of this death. This is a normal time of depression—of tears and feelings of helplessness. It's important during this stage to pour out your grief to friends, family, a pastor, and maybe your doctor.

5. The stage Oates calls "selective memory." You live in the real world without your loved one but then, all of a sudden, you will see a picture, hear a song, or experience something else which will trigger your grief once again and you will be down for a few hours or days.

6. The stage of recovery—a time of moving on with life. Your grief work is over and you start to live again.

To move through these stages from shock to recovery is to experience good grief. Unfortunately, some people never move to the stage of recovery. Some get stuck in depression, bitterness, or anger. Some people nurse their grief and do not allow themselves to get well. This is a serious problem because it becomes idolatry—putting a person at the center of your life.

A young man once wrote his friend, the great Reformer, Martin Luther. His wife had died, and he wanted to know what he should do at this point in his life. Luther told him to grieve, grieve, and then grieve some more. But Luther told him to finally put an end to his grief lest he become idolatrous and worship the dead instead of the living Lord. Luther reminded his friend that at some point one must put an end to their grief.

It takes time, however, to work through grief. I remember talking to a family who was concerned about their mother. She still grieved over the loss of her husband several months after his death. But she had been married to this man for over fifty years. You don't get over the death of your husband of fifty years in a few weeks or months. It takes several months to even a couple of years to totally work through grief. But a time must come for putting an end to grief and moving on with life.

Blessed

Jesus speaks of mourning in this verse. But He says, "Blessed are those who mourn." At first glance that sounds strange. Blessed? Mourning hurts. Grief is hard. How can it be a blessing?

But when you think about it, grief is a blessing. Think of why we grieve. It's because we've loved, because our life has been entwined with another, and we are richer and better for the relationship. The fact that we grieve means we've loved and the old saying is true—it's better to have loved and lost then to have never loved at all.

I learned about the blessing of grief when I turned thirteen. My grandmother had just died. I'll never forget the day of her funeral. My grandfather stood over her casket after the funeral service, weeping and deeply grieving. But he was also praying. I heard his words, "Thank You, Lord, for this wonderful woman. Thank You for the fifty-two years we loved each other. Thank You for the children we bore and raised." In spite of his great loss, my grandfather knew he was blessed because he had loved his wife and lived with her for so long.

So there is blessing in grief. I've done some hard funerals in my life, but in a way they have been a blessing because I've had the privilege of knowing and loving some good people. Blessed, said Jesus, are those who grieve.

Comforted

But that's not enough by itself. In grief we also need some relief. And so our Lord said, "For they shall be comforted." The good news is that God will help us through the experience of grief. He will give us comfort as we face our pain. In Psalm 23 the Bible speaks of walking through the valley of the shadow of death. Well, God helps us through, and does so in many ways. Let me review a few ways in which God comforts us when we grieve.

We can find comfort by remembering the *person* who has died. We can affirm that their life counted for good—that they enriched our life and the lives of others. At first, memories of our loved one can hurt because our wounds are still raw. But after awhile, when we recall the good memories of people whom we have loved, comfort comes.

God also comforts us through the *people* around us. When we grieve we need the strength of family and friends and church family. Words don't even have to be spoken—it's enough to just be there. When the space shuttle *Challenger* blew up, NASA sent space families to be with every family who lost a loved one. As one member of NASA said, "There's still nothing more powerful than one human being reaching out to another." When we grieve, God's grace is often mediated by the people around us.

A third way God sometimes brings comfort to us is through *professionals*. Sometimes grief leads to serious depression and you may need to see your doctor or seek counseling from your pastor. These people can be God's instruments to help you work through grief. Reading books by professionals on the subject is also helpful. Several such books are available in the church library. These books can help you if you are struggling with grief.

God also brings comfort through His *presence*. God is available to give us strength, power, and comfort in our deepest hurt and pain of grief. Prayer is so important—even if it's hard to pray. It's normal to feel abandoned at times—but God will not abandon us. He suffers with us as He suffered when His own Son died on the cross. God offers spiritual resources through His Spirit which can help us through the experience of grief. God would say to us in our grief: "My child I love you, I understand how you feel. I am near to love you, to listen to you, to comfort you, and to strengthen you." Keep on praying and worshiping and you will discover that God's strength will help you through the valley of the shadow of death and grief.

The last means of comfort I will mention is the *promise* of eternal life. The Bible says that we don't grieve as those who have no hope. We belong to the risen Christ—the resurrection and the life, and we have the hope and comfort of eternal life.

We have a great promise—that our loved ones are in the loving care of God—in a place where there are no more tears and where death is no more. And we will join them one day in that place for a great reunion.

"Blessed are those who mourn," says our Lord, "for they shall be comforted." And He does comfort us—in these ways and in others, so that we can move on and live again.

Many of you have read Catherine Marshall's books about her husband Peter Marshall. Upon his death, Catherine experienced deep grief. But she finally decided to have done with grief and get on with life without Peter and she wrote a book called *To Live Again.* And on this Memorial Day, that is the promise of God—that He will help you walk through your grief—and that you will be able to move on with life and that you, like Catherine Marshall, will live again. "Blessed are those who mourn, for they shall be comforted."

Notes

1. Harold Kushner, *When All You've Ever Wanted Isn't Enough: the Search for a Life that Matters* (New York: Pocket Books, 1986), 90-91.

2. Craig Selness, "Facing the Inevitable," *Christianity Today*, 7 October 1983, 41.

3. Wayne Oates, *Your Particular Grief* (Philadelphia: Westminster Press, 1981), 102-103.

8

Father's Day

As mentioned in the chapter on Mother's Day, I feel no obligation to observe Mother's Day or Father's Day. They do, however, provide an excellent opportunity to focus attention on the Christian family. A suggested order of worship for Father's Day follows. Like Mother's Day, the theme of the service comes from the hymn, "God, Give Us Christian Homes."

I've also included a marriage-renewal service. This can be a meaningful part of a Father's Day worship service.

The Worship of God

God, Give Us Christian Homes

Prelude
Call to Worship .... Children's Choir
The Greeting
Doxology
Invocation
Hymn .... God, Give Us Christian Homes .... No. 397

Homes Where the Father Is True and Strong

Recognition of Fathers
Scripture Reading .... Ephesians 5:25-32
Testimony

Homes Where the Bible Is Loved and Taught

Scripture Readings
Offertory Hymn . . . . . Word of God, Across the Ages . . . . . . No. 148
Offering

Homes Where the Master's Will Is Sought

Anthem . . . . The Gift of Love
Sermon . . . . A Father's Best Gift
Renewal of Marriage Vows
Invitation Hymn . . . . I Surrender All . . . . No. 347
Benediction
Postlude

Marriage-Renewal Ceremony

As a climax to this service, you might consider inviting couples to come forward for a renewal of their wedding vows. This could also be done earlier in the service, immediately after singing "God, Give Us Christian Homes."

The congregation should know several weeks in advance that this event is coming. This gives couples plenty of time to consider participating, as well as creates a positive sense of anticipation. A possible ceremony follows. You might want to print this as a bulletin insert in your order of worship. Begin the renewal of vows by inviting all who want to participate to come forward.

Introduction

You have come today to give thanks to God for His blessing upon your marriage, and to reaffirm your marriage covenant. As we prepare for this significant act of worship, let us seek God's blessings on this event through prayer.

Prayer

Dear Heavenly Father, thank You for these couples who come to renew the promises they have made to each other. Grant them Your blessings and grace, and help them honor and keep the promises and vows which they renew today. Fill this event with great meaning in their lives. Make this a special time in their pilgrimage of marriage. We pray in the name of Jesus Christ our Lord. Amen.

Renewal of Vows

The Book of Ruth has a beautiful passage which can illustrate the life-long commitment and love of marriage. In this account, Ruth says to Naomi: "Entreat me not to leave you or to return from following you; for where you go I will go, and where you lodge I will lodge; your people shall be my people and your God my God; where you die, I will die, and there will I be buried"(1:16-17). In this spirit of love and commitment will you please renew your vows. Please repeat after me:

Husbands: I renew my vows to you / to be your husband / to have and to hold/ from this day forward / for better for worse / for richer for poorer / in sickness and in health/ to love and to cherish / till death do we part. / This is my solemn vow.

Wives: I renew my vows to you / to be your wife / to have and to hold / from this day forward / for better for worse / for richer for poorer / in sickness and in health / to love and to cherish / till death do we part. / This is my solemn vow.

Prayer

Let us pray. Please repeat after me: We thank you most gracious God / for consecrating our marriage / in the name of Jesus Christ our Lord. / Lead us further in companionship / with each other and with You. / Give us grace to live together / in love and fidelity / with care for one another. / Through Jesus Christ our Lord. (Note: Worship leader may want to conclude this time of prayer with an additional individual prayer for the couples who have just renewed their vows.)

Benediction

May God the Father, who at creation ordained that man and woman become one flesh, keep you one.

May God the Son, who affirmed marriage by His first miracle at the wedding of Cana, be present with you always.

May God the Holy Spirit, who has given you the grace to persevere in your love and commitment to this point, strengthen your bond daily.

And may God, the source of all blessings, bless you this day and forever. Amen.

A Father's Best Gift
Ephesians 5:25-32

One day a little girl waited impatiently for her father to come home so the family could eat dinner. Finally, in exasperation she said, "Mommy, if the stork brings our babies, if Santa Claus brings all of our presents, if the Lord gives us our daily bread, and Uncle Sam our Social Security, why do we keep Daddy around?"

Today is Father's Day. I want to use this occasion to talk about Christian fathers, but in a somewhat different way. Rather than speaking about fathers loving their children, I want to focus on fathers loving their wives.

Several years ago, Zig Ziglar was chatting with his son. Zig asked him, "Son, if anybody should ask you what you like best about your dad, what would you say?" His son pondered for a moment and said, "I'd say the thing I like best about my dad is that he loves my mom."[1]

The point of today's sermon is simple. The best gift fathers can give their children is a healthy marriage. When fathers love their wives, their children reap great benefits. They feel safe and secure, they learn how to love and how to live. Fathers—love your wife, for this is the greatest gift you can give your children.

I heard a story about a husband who was a bit confused about this important subject. His wife suffered from depression and was always upset and unhappy. The concerned husband took her to a psychiatrist. The doctor listened to the couple talk about their relationship, and then said, "The treatment I prescribe is really quite simple." With that he went over to the man's wife, gathered her up in his arms, and gave her a big kiss. He then stepped back and looked at the woman's glowing face and broad smile. Turning to the woman's husband, he said: "See! All she needs is a little love. That will put new life back into her." Expressionless, the husband said, "Okay, Doc. I can bring her in on Tuesdays and Thursdays."[2]

Some time ago, a West German magazine released the fascinating results of a study conducted by a life-insurance company. This study found that husbands who kiss their wives every morning live an average of five years longer, are involved in fewer auto accidents, are ill 50 percent less time, and earn 20 to 30 percent more money.[3] Husbands, love your wives. It's good for you! It's also good for her and for your children.

There is a better motivation, however, for loving your wife—a biblical motivation. The Bible says, "Husbands, love your wives, as Christ loved the church and gave himself up for her" (Eph. 5:25). The same passage also says, "Even so husbands should love their wives as their own bodies" (v. 28).

When we love our wife as Christ loved the church, and when we love our wife as much as we love our own bodies, everyone is a winner—our wife, ourself, and our children. Christian fathers, the greatest gift we can give our children is to love our wives.

How should we love our wives? We're to love them like Christ loved the church. That's a lot of love. And Christ expressed His love in some very tangible ways. In what ways did Christ express His love to His church? Let's review a few of them.

Christ Made His Church a Priority

If we are to obey this command to love our wife as Christ loved the church, we must make our marriage a priority. James Dobson once said, "If America is going to survive, it will be because husbands and fathers begin to put their families at the highest level of priorities and reserve something of their time, effort, and energy for leadership within their own homes."

There are many important things in life—our jobs, our friends, our church. But after God, our number-one priority must be our marriage and our family. This is true even of pastors. You've heard people comment about a busy pastor, "he's married to the church." Well, that's a tragedy. And it's also sick theology. The only groom of the church is Jesus Christ. If a pastor is married to the church he is living in great sin.

A pastor, like all husbands, is married to his wife. Not his job, not his outside interests—his wife! Many men succeed at their career, but if it's at the expense of their marriage and family, they are failures. Fathers, if we are to love our wives as Christ loves the church, we must make our marriage a priority.

Christ Gave His Church His Time

Jesus spent many years with His church. If we are to love our wife as Christ loved the church, we are going to have to give her our time. We've heard the cliche before, but it's true. How do you spell love? You spell it T-I-M-E. When we spend time with our wives, developing our marriage, our children will be blessed.

Christ Served His Church

It's amazing to read how Jesus, the Son of Almighty God, washed the feet of His disciples, and how He died for our sin. If we are to love our wives as Christ loved the church, we must meet their needs. We must serve them the best we can.

Christ Had Affection for His Church

You cannot read the New Testament without seeing this truth. The church is even called the "Bride of Christ." Jesus deeply loves His church. He feels affection for His church. If we are to love our wives as Christ loved the church, we must show them affection.

Women need affection from their husbands. Husbands need to express that affection both verbally and physically. We need to tell them that we love them, that they are beautiful, that we appreciate them. We also need to hold and hug them. I once heard a woman psychologist say, "Every woman needs at least one big hug a day."

"Husbands," says the Bible, "love your wives as Christ loved the church." Make her a priority, give her your time, serve her, show her some affection. She will benefit, you will benefit, and your children will benefit. Loving your wife is the best thing you can do for your children.

I can almost hear some of you say, "But, Preacher, you don't know my wife and my marriage. It's hard to love her. I don't feel like loving her anymore. The spark is gone. We're struggling to just stay together."

That reminds me of a story. A man named Pete was unhappy with his marriage. He no longer saw his wife as interesting, fun to be with, attractive, or someone he wanted to continue living with. She had become a sloppy housekeeper, overweight, and had developed a nit-picking, fault-finding personality. Overwhelmed with it all, Pete sought advice from a divorce attorney. Not only did Pete want out of the marriage, he wanted advice on how to hurt her. He wanted to make life miserable for his soon-to-be ex-wife.

The attorney listened to Pete's story and then offered this advice: "Pete, I have the perfect plan for you. When you get home this afternoon, I want you to begin treating your wife like a queen. I mean a queen! Do everything in your power to serve her, please her, and make her feel like royalty. Listen to her every thought with sincerity, give her a hand around the house, take her out for a few unexpected candlelight dinners, and even pick up flowers for her on your way from work. Then, after two or three months of this royal treatment, just pack your bags and leave her. That will surely get to her. In fact, I can't think of anything that would hurt more than that."

Pete thought about the advice for a few moments. "It sounds like a great plan. She would never expect anything like this from me." Pete couldn't wait to get home and get started. He even picked up a dozen roses on his way home. That night, he helped his wife with the dinner dishes and then brought her breakfast in bed the next morning.

Pete began complimenting her on her clothes, cooking, and housekeeping habits. The two of them even went on a weekend getaway.

After three weeks, Pete received a call from his divorce attorney. "Pete," he said, "I have the divorce papers ready if you are ready. In a matter of minutes, we can make you a happy bachelor again."

"Are you kidding?" Pete responded. "Why, I am married to an absolute queen. You wouldn't believe the changes she has made. In fact, her attitude and behavior have made a complete turnaround. I wouldn't divorce her in a million years."[4]

Marriage isn't easy. It's hard work to keep a marriage healthy, but it's worth it. A good marriage makes for a happy home and well-adjusted children. And what's the key? It's found in our text today, "Husbands, love your wives as Christ loved the church."

Do you remember the classic movie, *Camelot*? In one scene, King Arthur is trying to remember Merlin's advice about how to handle a woman. He's struggling with his marriage, and doesn't know what to do. Arthur says to himself, "How to handle a woman? There's a way said the wise old man." Then he remembered Merlin's wise advice on this subject. Merlin once told him the secret: love her, simply love her.

"Husbands, love your wives, as Christ loved the church."

"Even so husbands should love their wives as their own bodies."

And this my friends, is the greatest gift you can ever give to your children.

Notes

1. *Pulpit Helps*, July 1987, Vol. 8, No. 6.
2. *The Pastor's Story File*, July 1987, Vol. 3, No. 9.
3. *The Lamplighter*, June 1988, Vol. 3, No. 6, 8.
4. Ibid.

9

Independence Day

Independence Day offers the church an opportunity to celebrate our national freedom. Offering thanks to God for our country is in order at this time of the year. Care must be taken, however, that we do not equate patriotism with Christian discipleship. The focus of our worship must be God, not America.

The Worship of God

A Celebration of Freedom

Freedom to Praise

Enter to Worship
Prelude
Choral Call to Worship...... Good News America, God Loves You
Responsive Reading.................................. No. 522
Hymn .... Come, Thou Almighty King........... No. 2
Invocation

Freedom to Pray

Hymn .... America the Beautiful............. No. 508
Discipline of Silence
Prayer of Thanksgiving
Hymn .... My Country, 'Tis of Thee........... No. 511
Offertory Prayer
Offering........................ Battle Hymn of the Republic

Freedom to Proclaim

Presentation of Colors
Testimony..................... What My Country Means to Me
Scripture Readings
Anthem......... Mine Eyes Have Seen the Glory.......... Choir
Sermon .... Let Freedom Ring.............. Pastor

Freedom to Serve

Hymn of Invitation .... Trusting Jesus .... No. 441
Choral Benediction .... God Bless America
Benediction
Depart to Serve

The above order of worship is an upbeat celebration of freedom. While appropriate for an Independence Day worship service, that should not be the focus every year. As Christians, we are citizens of two kingdoms. Our loyalty to God, however, is greater than our loyalty to country. Independence Day offers a good opportunity to reflect on this dual citizenship. The following order of worship can help you develop that theme. The sermon would be based on Matthew 22:15-22. It should point out responsibilities to our country and our responsibilities to God.

The Worship of God

Prelude
Responsive Reading No. 521
Doxology
Invocation

Render unto Caesar

Hymn .... My Country, 'Tis of Thee .... No. 511
Presentation of Flags
Pledge to the American Flag
Hymn .... America the Beautiful.............. No. 508
Prayer of Thanksgiving
Testimony

Solo.. Statue of Liberty

Render unto God

Old Testament Reading......................... Isaiah 40:15-23
New Testament Reading...................... Matthew 22:15-22
Hymn .... I Love Thy Kingdom, Lord .... No. 240
Offering
Pledge to the Christian Flag
Chorus .... He Is Lord
Choral Anthem .... Glorious Is Thy Name Most Holy
Sermon ...... Render Unto Caesar, Render Unto God...... Pastor
Hymn of Invitation .... I Am Thine, O Lord......... No. 352
Benediction
Postlude

Let Freedom Ring

This morning, I read an uncensored newspaper because this country believes in freedom of the press. I then came to this church to study the Bible and worship because this country believes in freedom of religion. I now stand before you and speak openly because this country believes in freedom of speech. And these are just a few of the freedoms we enjoy in America.

We in the United States are blessed in many ways. We have tremendous natural resources, great scenic beauty, a basically strong economy, good health care, a strong education system. But our greatest blessing is freedom. Because it's so common to us, so familiar, it's easy to take freedom for granted and forget how fortunate we are.

Like many of you, I was deeply moved by the events in China in 1989. When students asked their government for more freedom, they received bullets instead. Millions of people across this globe don't even begin to enjoy the freedom which we have in America.

Let me note a word of caution, however. We must be careful in our praise for America. We are here to worship God, not our country. This country has many faults. As Christian citizens, we ought to improve our country when it is wrong.

In spite of its faults, this country has many things for which we should be grateful. There is much about America that we can celebrate. Freedom, however, is the most important.

Freedom and liberty are important to this country. Our nation was born out of a vision of freedom. Our Declaration of Independence reads, "All men are created equal, that they are endowed by their Creator with certain unalienable rights." Our Constitution tells us that the reason for establishing the United States was to "Secure the blessings of liberty to ourselves and our posterity." As Lincoln said at Gettysburg, our nation was "conceived in liberty."

Because freedom and liberty are important to us, we have many symbols of that freedom. We sing songs, for example, which say things like, "My country 'tis o thee, Sweet land of liberty." We have a Liberty Bell. We have a *Statue of Liberty*.

Freedom is a priority for us. It's important to us. I would remind you, however, that freedom is also important to God. God is a God of freedom. We see that truth throughout the Bible. In the Old Testament, the people of Israel were oppressed slaves in Egypt. God sent Moses to liberate the people and set them free through the exodus.

In the New Testament we once again see people enslaved, captive to the power of sin. God saw the human race in bondage to sin so He sent Christ to set us free.

God is a God of freedom. Our forefathers understood that. That knowledge inspired the fathers of this country to create a land of liberty.

Freedom is a great gift and we are blessed with it in wonderful abundance in this country. But we must always remember—there is a cost to freedom.

On July 4, 1776, our country declared its independence and liberty— but at a great cost. Our forefathers experienced suffering—blood, sweat, tears, and agony at places like Lexington, Bunker Hill, Georgetown, Yorktown, and Valley Forge. But that was just the beginning. We have continued to pay the price throughout our history. In World War I that cost was over 115,000 American soldiers killed in action. In World War II the cost was over 400,000 soldiers. We have paid dearly for our freedom and we must always be willing to pay the price.

Freedom is a great thing. We enjoy much of it in America. So it is appropriate that on this day of worship we thank God for our freedom, and that we commit ourselves to preserving our liberty so that freedom will always ring from sea to shining sea.

In 1833 the British Parliament voted to abolish slavery in Jamaica. As the effective date of freedom drew near, excitement and anticipation grew among the slaves. The night before their freedom was to begin, the slaves of Jamaica did not sleep. Rather, they dressed in their best clothes and went to the mountainsides to catch the first glimpse of dawn on their first day of freedom. As the first rays of sunlight streaked across the horizon, the slaves erupted in irrepressible ecstasy, "Free at last, free at last, Thank God Almighty, we're free at last!"

10

Thanksgiving

The Worship of God

Great Is the Lord, and Greatly to Be Praised
(Ps. 145:3)

Prelude
Choral Call to Worship....... Now Let Us All Praise God and Sing
Responsive Reading No. 626
Hymn .... We Gather Together .... No. 229
Invocation

The Lord Is Near to All Who Call upon Him
(Ps. 145:18)

Duet .... O Give Thanks to the Lord
Discipline of Silence
Prayer of Thanksgiving................................ Pastor

One Generation Shall Laud Thy Works to Another
(Ps. 145:4)

Testimony........................ Giving Thanks for My Family
Hymn .... Sing to the Lord of Harvest .... No. 232
Testimony................ Giving Thanks for My Church Family

The Lord Is Gracious and Merciful
(Ps. 145:8)

Hymn .... Come, Ye Thankful People, Come .... No. 233
Offertory Prayer
Offering

My Mouth Will Speak the Praise of the Lord
(Ps. 145:21)

Scripture Reading .... 1 Thessalonians 5:18
Anthem............ A Hymn for Thanksgiving .... Choir
Sermon .... Giving Thanks in All Circumstances .... Pastor
Hymn .... For the Beauty of the Earth........... No. 49
Benediction.................................... The Doxology
Postlude

An Optional Thanksgiving Service

Another possible worship service for Thanksgiving is a service of testimonies, Scripture reading, and music. Rather than a sermon, numerous people could share testimonies and read Scripture. The service would also have lots of music. Consider having the children's choirs sing, as well as having soloists, duets, quartets, choir numbers, and so forth. Divide the service into several segments such as:

GIVING THANKS FOR SALVATION
GIVING THANKS FOR FAMILY AND FRIENDS
GIVING THANKS FOR CHURCH
GIVING THANKS FOR THE GROWTH OF STRUGGLES

Under each segment of worship include an appropriate testimony, a Scripture reading, and some form of music—hymn, chorus, solo, quartet, choral number, and so forth. This kind of service will be well received by your congregation. Other Thanksgiving worship ideas can be found on pages 138-139 and 226 of *Getting Ready for Sunday: A Practical Guide for Worship Planning.*

Giving Thanks in All Circumstances
1 Thess. 5:18

A woman went to visit one of her friends. Her six-year-old son, Johnny, went with her. When he complained of hunger, the woman's friend offered little Johnny an orange. Immediately after the woman gave him the orange, Johnny's mother said, "Now what do you say?" Johnny looked at the orange, handed it back to the woman, and said, "Peel it."

Unfortunately, many of us, like Johnny, don't do so well at being thankful. Gratitude, however, is an important attitude if we want to be happy. Several years ago a magazine publisher polled a number of prominent people all over the world to see what they desired most. Many interesting answers came in. A noted writer wished for health. One public official said, "Give me a little Vermont farm with a brook and an apple orchard and I'll be satisfied." A gifted author wanted the ability to understand the language of animals. The best answer, however, came from a man who said, "What I desire most of all is an ever greater ability to appreciate what I already have."[1]

During this Thanksgiving holiday. I want to talk to you about gratitude. In our text for today, the apostle Paul said, "In every thing give thanks: for this is the will of God in Christ Jesus concerning you"(KJV).

Please note that this verse does not say that everything that happens to you is God's will. It says that it's God's will for you to always give thanks. The *New International Version* translates this verse, "Give thanks in all circumstances, for this is God's will for you in Christ Jesus." The circumstances may not be God's will—but it is His will that you be a thankful person.

Paul was an expert in this kind of gratitude. He experienced all kinds of circumstances—many of them negative. He worked for years under adverse circumstances: persecution, physical torture, shipwrecks, and imprisonment. Yet, in all of these circumstances, Paul wrote again and again about thankfulness and gratitude.

To the Romans he wrote, "I thank my God through Jesus Christ"(1:8). To the church at Philippi, where he was imprisoned and beaten, he said, "I thank my God on every remembrance of you"(1:3,

KJV). To the church at Corinth, who caused him all kinds of heartaches and headaches, he wrote, "I thank my God always on your behalf"(1 Cor 1:4, KJV). To Timothy he said, "I thank God whom I serve, . . . when I remember you constantly in my prayers"(2 Tim. 1:3). To the church at Ephesus he wrote, "Giving thanks always for all things unto God"5:20, KJV). Ephesus is where they rioted and drove him out of town, where he was unjustly accused and persecuted, yet he was still thankful for his experience there. In today's text, this letter to the church in Thessalonica, he declared, "in every thing give thanks"(1 Thess. 5:18, KJV).

Paul's life was a life of gratitude. And then came the day for his death. The soldiers unlocked the chains and took him outside the walls of Rome to execute him. They said "Paul, put your head down." He put his head down on the chopping block and they prepared to sever his head from his body with an axe. At that moment we can almost hear Paul say, "Thanks be to God that I can die for Christ." Paul had perpetual thanksgiving.

And in today's text, Paul declared that we also should be people of gratitude. "In every thing give thanks." It's not a suggestion, it's a command. It's God's will for us.

This means that gratitude and thankfulness are a choice. We choose to be grateful or to be resentful. It's our decision.

Dr. Victor Frankl, the bold, courageous Jew who became a prisoner during the Holocaust, and endured years of indignity and humiliation by the Nazis before he was finally liberated. At the beginning of his ordeal, he was marched into a Gestapo courtroom. His captors had taken away his home and family, his cherished freedom, his possessions, even his watch and wedding ring. They shaved his head and stripped him. There he stood before the German high command, naked under glaring lights, being interrogated and falsely accused. He was destitute, a helpless pawn in the hands of brutal, prejudiced, sadistic men. He had nothing. But no—he knew that wasn't true. He suddenly realized there was one thing no one could ever take from him—just one. Frankl realized he still had the power to choose his own response. No matter what anyone would ever do to him, regardless of what the future held for him, the response was his to make. Bitterness or forgiveness? Give up or go on? Hatred or hope? The paralysis of self-pity or the determination to endure?[2]

Paul, like Frankl, knew many horrible circumstances. But he continued to choose gratitude over resentment. And he told us to do the same.

I heard the following story at a Lion's Club meeting. A woman in Arkansas started going blind while carrying her last child. She was totally blind at his birth and lived in blindness for almost twenty years. Her boy joined the military and was soon stationed overseas. About that time, a Lion's club member referred her to a Lion's Club eye clinic. The doctors performed a simple, twenty-minute operation on her eyes. Afterwards, she gained full sight in one eye and partial sight in the other. When her son returned from overseas, she saw him for the first time in her life.

The response at the Lion's Club meeting proved interesting. Some of the members said, "That's awful. She was blind all those years when all she needed was a simple operation to cure her. What a horrible waste of twenty years." However, others said, "Isn't it wonderful that she can see again! Isn't it great that she can once again enjoy eyesight—see her son, see the world again!" Two very different responses.

I'd like to meet that woman. I wonder what attitude she chose—resentment that she was unnecessarily blind for twenty years, or gratitude that she could now see again.

You see, it's always our choice. Every situation is a mixture of good and bad. God says, make the gratitude choice. See what there is to be thankful for rather than dwelling on the negative things.

When Robinson Crusoe was wrecked on his lonely island, he drew two columns and listed the good and bad of his situation. He was cast on a desolate island, but he was still alive. He was divided from mankind, but he was not starving. He had no clothes, but was in a warm climate and didn't need them. He had no means of defense, but saw no wild beasts which threatened him. He had no one to talk to, but the destroyed ship was near the shore and he could get out of it all the things necessary for his basic needs. He concluded, therefore, that no condition in the world was so miserable that one could not find something to be grateful for.

When John Claypool lost his ten-year-old daughter to leukemia, gratitude was the only way he survived. His struggle is told in his little book, *Tracks of a Fellow Struggler*. He said he tried three different paths after his little girl died. The first was to say, "Well, it was just God's will. I have to accept it." But that was no good. He could not believe that God willed ten-year-old girls to die of leukemia. A second path was to try to find an intellectual answer as to why this happened. He tried to make sense of it. But that didn't work either—this death didn't make any sense. Finally, Claypool took the path of gratitude. He realized that life is a gift. We are not entitled to it. He chose to be thankful for the ten good years they had together rather than be consumed with resentment for the years he did not have with her. This path of gratitude wasn't easy, but it was the only path which offered any help.

Such was the apostle Paul's way. He was no shallow optimist or positive attitude thinker. He knew the hard realities of suffering. But Paul choose to be grateful rather than be resentful. There are always bad things in life, but there are always good things as well. Paul says, concentrate on the good. Be grateful even in difficult circumstances. There is always something to be thankful for. Paul chose gratitude rather than resentment.

This is what our Pilgrim forefathers did back in 1621. You have heard many times how that little band of Puritans set out on the *Mayflower* for Virginia, only to get blown off course and finally come to shore hundreds of miles to the north at Cape Cod. The winter was much worse than they anticipated, and by April only fifty of the original 102 had survived. A discussion arose as to whether those remaining should give up and go back to the Old World, but they decided to stay and plant one more crop—a few acres of corn and barley. When the time of the first anniversary of their landing rolled around, discussion arose as to how it should be observed. Some proposed a day of mourning when attention would be focused on all those who lay in unmarked graves in foreign soil. But the others said, "No, a day of thanksgiving would be more appropriate. After all, fifty of us have survived. We have gathered in a good harvest. The Indians have been our friends. Let's focus on what we have going for us, not on what we have going against us."

"In all things give thanks." This is God's will but it's our choice. We must decide whether to be resentful or to have gratitude in life. God wants us to develop an attitude of gratitude. I visited a woman with such an attitude just this week. She is terribly sick. Her situation is bad. Yet she said to me, "I'm so thankful to have my family with me during this struggle." She knows how to do God's will and give thanks in all things.

Oh, I can hear the critics. "Preacher," you might say, "you just don't know my situation. Things are horrible. How can I be grateful?"

Such a question reminds me of an old story with which I'll close today's sermon. There was an elderly English pastor who was famous for his pulpit prayers. He always found something to thank God for, even in bad times. One stormy Sunday morning, when everything was going extremely bad in the community and in the lives of many people, he stepped to the pulpit to pray. A member of the congregation thought to himself, *The preacher will have nothing to thank God for on a wretched morning like this.* The pastor began his prayer, "We thank Thee, O God that it is not always like this."

Hear again the word of God, "give thanks in all circumstances; for this is the will of God in Christ Jesus for you."

Another Sermon Idea

Luke 24:13-35 offers a good sermon possibility. This, of course, is the familiar Easter story of the disciples and Jesus on the road to Emmaus. The disciples did not recognize Jesus. We don't know why. Many theories exist. Perhaps the best answer lies in the mystery of the resurrected body of Jesus Christ. Regardless, when Jesus offered a prayer of gratitude for the evening meal, the disciples recognized Him. The sermon could be called, "Known by His Gratitude." In the sermon we can challenge our congregation to be known by their gratitude, to be people who truly give thanks in all circumstances. Observing the Lord's Supper would be appropriate for this Thanksgiving service.

Notes

1. Brian Harbour, *From Cover to Cover* (Nashville: Broadman Press, 1982), 210.
2. Chuck Swindoll, *Strengthening Your Grip* (Waco, Tex.: Word Books, no date given), 206.

Part III
Special Sundays from the Denominational Calendar

11

Race Relations Sunday

As a young pastor in Arkansas, I dreaded Race Relations Day. I knew I didn't have to observe Race Relations Sunday, but I also knew that my church needed to observe it.

Race relations are still strained in many places. We desperately need to hear God's message on the subject and grapple with the implications.

Although a few people got angry, observing Race Relations Day every year was basically a good experience for me and my congregation. If handled with sensitivity, Race Relations Day can be a positive experience of worship and growth. It calls us to God's ideal of breaking down racial barriers. It reminds us how far we are from His ideal, and forces us to confess our sin and strive for wholeness in this area. It challenges us to grow in our love for others, even those we've been taught to fear and hate. It helps broaden our hearts and minds. Race Relations Day is an appropriate focus of worship. I encourage you to observe this special day.

Some churches have experimented with a pulpit exchange on Race Relations Day. The white minister preaches in the black church and the black minister preaches in the white church. If you can overcome initial resistance to this concept, it can be a wonderful experience. Some white churches invite a black choir to perform on this day or even have a choir exchange. Although these are good ideas, I realize that many churches are not yet ready for this experience. Such ideas are not necessary, however, for an effective Race Relations Day. The following order of worship and sermon summary could be used anywhere.

The Worship of God

And one of them, a lawyer, asked him a question, to test him. "Teacher, which is the great commandment in the law?" And he said to him, "You shall love the Lord your God with all your heart, and with all your soul, and with all your mind. This is the great and first commandment. And a second is like it, You shall love your neighbor as yourself. On these two commandments depend all the law and the prophets" (Matt. 22:35-40).

You Shall Love the Lord Your God

Prelude
Chorus .... O Come Let Us Adore Him
Hymn .... Crown Him with Many Crowns .... No. 52
Invocation
Testimony
Offertory Hymn .... I Love Thee .... No. 75
Offering

You Shall Love Your Neighbor as Yourself

The Greeting
Chorus .... Bond of Love
Selected Scripture Readings
Prayer of Confession
Hymn .... In Christ There Is No East or West .... No. 258
Solo .... Christ Is the World's True Light
Sermon .... Remember the Dream
Invitation Hymn ..... Have Thine Own Way, Lord ...... No. 349
Benediction
Postlude

Remember the Dream

During the civil-rights march in Washington in 1963 Martin Luther King, Jr. stood in front of thousands of people and shared his dream.

"I have a dream" said King, "that my four little children will one day live in a nation where they will not be judged by the color of their skin but by the content of their character. I have a dream today. I have a dream that one day little black boys and black girls will be able to join hands with little white boys and white girls and walk together as sisters and brothers. I have a dream today."

Five years later, on April 4, 1968 in Memphis, Tennessee, Martin Luther King, age thirty-nine, was assassinated. Racial violence followed and continues even today. We are a long way from realizing Martin Luther King's dream.

Why do we still have race problems? The fact that we even observe a Race Relations Day shows that we have a racial problem in this country. Why haven't we done better on this subject? It's certainly not the Bible's fault. The Bible makes it very clear that racism of any type is wrong.

The Bible Condemns Racism

Whatever we say about race relations, we cannot say that God is happy with our situation. The Bible clearly shows that God wants us to get along with all persons. Consider just a few biblical principles which relate to race relations.

1. All humans are a single family and have a common origin. In Acts 17:26 we read, "And [God] made from one every nation of men to live on all the face of the earth."

2. Humanity was created in the image of God and has infinite worth. Genesis 1:27 says, "So God created man in his own image, in the image of God he created him; male and female he created them."

3. Jesus died for every person regardless of race. John 3:16 says, "For God so loved the world, that he gave his only begotten Son"(KJV).

4. Believers of all races are the family of God. Ephesians 4:4-6 says, "There is one body and one Spirit, . . . one Lord, one faith, one baptism, one God and Father of us all."

5. God is no respecter of persons. All people are of equal value to Him. As we read in Romans 2:11, "God shows no partiality."

6. The gospel abolishes human barriers which separate race against race. In Ephesians 2:14 we read, "For he is our peace, who has made us both one, and has broken down the dividing wall of hostility." The same principle is seen in Galatians 3:28, "There is neither Jew nor Greek, there

is neither slave nor free, there is neither male nor female; for you are all one in Jesus Christ."

7. The principle of *agape* love condemns racism. First John 4:8 says, "He who does not love does not know God; for God is love."

8. And finally, we see this principle in the great commandment, "You shall love your neighbor as yourself."

The Bible is absolutely clear. God hates racism. Our problem is not with the Bible but with ourselves.

Racism Still Exists

In spite of what God says in His word, we still have a race problem. We have a problem in our country and we have a problem in our community.

I could cite many examples. Just this week the newspaper had stories about the growing violence of the KKK. I could talk about many instances in our own town where racism continues to raise its ugly head. I could remind you of instances of racism in our own church.

We don't have to look far, do we? We don't have to look any further than our own hearts. Each of us, to some degree, struggles with racism. I don't pretend that I'm free of prejudice. I'm not. None of us are. But that doesn't change the fact that racism is a sin. It's wrong. God wants us to change our hatred into love, our fear into understanding. But how?

God Can Help Us Overcome Racism

I didn't come to church today to antagonize you. I didn't come here to condemn. I came to proclaim hope. If we'll let Him, God will help us overcome our sin of racism.

Our problem isn't new. All through history, people have had a hard time getting along with people different from themselves. In Jesus' day the problem was not blacks and whites but Jews and Gentiles.

One of my favorite stories in the New Testament comes from the fourth chapter of John. In this passage, Jesus confronts the disciples with their sin of racism.

You remember the story. Jesus told the disciples that He "must needs go through Samaria"(v.4, KJV). The disciples hated Samaritans. They couldn't believe He was actually going to go to Samaria. Grady Nutt, in his little book, *The Gospel According to Norton,*[1] retells the story with insight and humor. I'd like to read two brief passages from his book.

> Jesus caught us all off guard . . . and headed right for Samaria! Simon almost developed a permanent twitch! He argued loud, long, and climaxed his furious debate with an unbelievable burst of logic: "But there are *Samaritans* up there!" to which Jesus responded:. . . "So . . .?" Simon looked from frantic face to frantic face and finally came up with: "Well . . . they just hide behind rocks waiting to leap out and be Samaritans right in front of you!" Jesus finally dropped his head as tears of laughter welled up in his eyes. . . .[2]

Well, Jesus not only went to Samaria, but He talked to a Samaritan—a woman Samaritan and a sinner at that. He even ate their food. Listen again to Grady Nutt.

> Jesus sat down . . . [by the well] . . . and said: "I'm hungry . . ."
> Simon almost passed out! "If we'd gone around we could have found food." Jesus was sure there'd be food here. "In *Samaria*?" shouted Simon . . . "In Samaria. . . ." Simon and his friends returned with a fish at arm's length. Jesus teased him again a little and pointed out that if that Samaritan fish had made it thirty miles further down the Jordan river he'd have been Jewish![3]

You know the story. Jesus went to their town and even stayed two more days. The result? Many people believed and the disciples learned an important lesson in race relations.

Of course, the lesson didn't completely take. Later, in Acts 10, we find Peter struggling with the whole issue all over again. But God is patient. He helped Peter understand that all people are equal and valuable and that they are loved by God and should be loved by God's children.

If we'll let Him, God will help us overcome our racism, just as He did for Peter. Slowly, if we want, we can leave the sin of racism behind. The gospel is big enough to overcome our prejudice and fear and hatred.

How do we do this? First, we admit that we are racists, every one of us. Second, we ask God to forgive us of our sin. Third, we believe what the Bible says about this subject. Fourth, we ask God to help us overcome our feelings of racism. Finally, we need to get to know people of other races and learn that we can love them and even like them.

Years ago, a young missionary went to Japan. He tried to serve the people as a minister of the gospel, but he struggled with prejudice. How could he be a missionary to people he didn't like? His racism bothered him. Finally, he went to an older, wiser missionary. He asked, "How can I learn to love all the Japanese people?" The wise old missionary said, "Begin by loving just one."

Step by step, with God's help, we can break down the barriers which separate us from others.

On the day before he was assassinated, Martin Luther King Jr. made a speech. In that speech he said: "I don't know what will happen now. We have got difficult days ahead. But it doesn't matter with me because I've been to the mountaintop. Like anyone else, I would like to live a long life. But I'm not concerned with that. I just want to do God's will and He has allowed me to go up the mountain. I see the promised land. I may not get there with you, but I want you to know tonight that as a people we will get to the promised land. I am happy tonight that I am not worried about anything. I'm not fearing any man. Mine eyes have seen the glory of the coming of the Lord."

The title of my sermon today is "Remember the Dream." It's not just Martin Luther King's dream—it is the dream of Jesus Christ and God the Father. It should be the dream of all Christians everywhere.

And if we'll try—if we'll take some risks and take some concrete steps—someday the dream will come true. One day, if we'll let it happen, we can all join hands with little white children and little black children and sing from our hearts, "Red and yellow, black and white, They are precious in His sight; Jesus loves the little children of the world."

Notes

1. Grady Nutt, *The Gospel According to Norton* (Nashville: Broadman Press, 1974).

2. Ibid, 38.

3. Ibid, 42-43.

12

World Hunger Day

World hunger is one of the great tragedies of our time. It demands a compassionate response from Christians. One small way to respond is to observe World Hunger Day every year in your church. It reminds us that while we have plenty to eat, others do not. It calls us to care. It challenges us to act on behalf of hungry people.

Caring for the poor and hungry is a major biblical concern. It was also a priority for Jesus. We would do well to address this subject in our worship and preaching. World Hunger Day provides a means to do so.

Worship Ideas

The Worship of God

"Pour Yourself Out for the Hungry"
(Isa. 58:10)

Take Delight in the Lord (Isa. 58:14)

Prelude
Choral Call to Worship
Hymn . . . . All Creatures of Our God and King . . . . No. 9
Invocation
Anthem . . . . Psalm 103 . . . . Choir
Chorus . . . . He Is Lord
Discipline of Silence
The Lord's Prayer

Hymn . . . . I Gave My Life for Thee . . . . No. 417
Offering

Share Your Bread with the Hungry (Isa. 58:7)

Responsive Reading. . . . . No. 587
Children's Sermon
Scripture Reading . . . . Matthew 14:13-21
Solo . . . . People to People
Sermon . . . . Give Them Something to Eat
Invitation Hymn . . . . I Surrender All . . . . No. 347
World Hunger Offering
Benediction
Postlude

You can find another order of worship for World Hunger Day on page 20 of *Getting Ready for Sunday: A Practical Guide for Worship Planning.*

The Offering

Many options exist for giving to world hunger. The most obvious is to observe a special world hunger offering. Another option is to order plastic rice bowl banks and distribute one to each family. Ask families to place the rice bowls on their kitchen table for the next four to six weeks. It will remind them that many do not have full tables and that they should be thankful for their food. Ask them to regularly place money in the bank. At the end of the allotted time, have a gathering of the banks. I did this several years when I was a pastor and an incredible amount of money was raised for world hunger.

A third possibility is to have an offering of letters to congressmen and senators. In these letters, ask public officials to do more for hungry people in our country and around the world. *Bread for the World*, a Christian hunger organization, would be happy to give you complete information on how to carry out an offering of letters. Another option is to collect nonperishable foods for a local organization who ministers to hungry people. Perhaps your church has a food bank. If so, the food could be used to restock the shelves.

Observe the Lord's Supper

A meaningful and significant World Hunger Day worship service could revolve around the Lord's Supper. The service would help American Christians confess that we are spiritually hungry and desperately need Jesus, the Bread of Life. It could then challenge us to share the Bread of Life with others in both spiritual and physical ways.

Preaching Ideas

Give Them Something to Eat
Matthew 14:13-21

A pastor returned from a tour of mission sites in the Far East and then visited area churches with his slide presentation. He had one particularly striking shot of a little girl, dressed in rags and obviously underfed, staring into a bakery window on a Hong Kong street. He used the slide to illustrate the need for more mission support.

After one such presentation, an observer remained behind. When he and the pastor were alone, he asked, "What did you do for that little girl?" It struck this pastor for the first time: he had not done anything. He took her picture and walked away. The change in his pocket would have fed her for weeks, but he hadn't done anything.

We've all seen pictures of the hungry—on television, in magazines, in newspapers. The question comes to us as well, "What have we done about it?" That's the issue of today's text. Let's look at it again.

A Problem Arose (vv. 14-15)

A great throng of hungry people gathered around Jesus. In our world today, a great throng of hungry people also exist.

It's hard to comprehend the magnitude of this problem. World hunger is an awesome nightmare. Up to 20 million people a year die from world hunger. I could give you statistics about how many die per day, per hour, per minute. I could talk about the number of children who die every week across the globe because they don't have enough to eat. But statistics are cold. They don't tell the real picture. I'm not talking about statistics but about real people. Real fathers and mothers who are in agony because they cannot feed their children. People like Bill, a poor man in Brazil. He and his family live in the slums and are hungry every day of the week. A missionary reported Bill saying: "Sometimes I think, if I die I won't have to see my children suffering as they are. Sometimes I even think of killing myself. So often I see them crying, hungry, and there I am, without a cent to buy them some bread. I think, *My God, I can't face it. I'll end my life. I don't want to look anymore.*"

We have a problem today. Hungry people are everywhere. And it's a complicated problem. There is enough food. God's creation produces enough food for everyone. It just doesn't get distributed evenly. Many factors cause world hunger: weather variations, overpopulation, economic and political injustice, poverty, unfair trade practices, the arms race, apathy, and people who feel helpless—who think the problem is so big, nothing can be done. Whatever the causes, there is a problem. Like the story in our text, a throng of hungry people surround us.

A Decision Was Made (v. 16)

The people were hungry. A decision had to be made. What would Jesus and the disciples do?

In the text, we see two options for resolving the problem—the way of the disciples or the way of Jesus. The disciples' way was to send them away. They didn't want to deal with these hungry people.

I can relate. Hunger is an unpleasant problem. When I see hunger-ridden people on television or in a magazine picture, I don't like to look. It makes me uncomfortable. Like the disciples, I want to say, "Lord, send them away."

A few years ago, I saw a youth group present a play on World Hunger Day. The setting was a restaurant in Mexico City. Although it was a fine restaurant, it was close to a slum area. A group of tourists had just been served, their plates filled with wonderful food. About that time, two children from the slums stood at the window and watched the group eat. The group felt uncomfortable seeing these two poor, dirty, hungry children stare at them through the window. Finally, one of the women in the group stood up and closed the curtain. They then finished their dinner.

That's what the disciples wanted to do. And I don't blame them. It's no fun seeing hungry people. "Send [them away]," they told Jesus. But Jesus would not send them away. Jesus' way was different from the disciples. Jesus said, "Give them something to eat"(vv.15-16).

"Give them something to eat." It's so simple. Jesus saw the need and He said, "Let's feed them."

I believe Jesus would say the same thing to us today. As we see the throngs of hungry people, Jesus again says, "Give them something to eat."

Caring for the poor, feeding the hungry—this is a biblical mandate. For Christians, it's not an option. We have a problem—people are hungry. We must decide, therefore, to give them something to eat.

A Strategy Was Developed (vv. 17-19a)

Next, Jesus developed a strategy. There was a problem—people were hungry. His decision was to give them something to eat. So He devised a strategy to feed them. He asked the disciples to discover what resources were available. They scouted around and found five loaves of bread and two fish. Jesus asked the people to sit down in groups and had His disciples distribute the food.

Millions of people are hungry today. We must develop a strategy to help. It's complicated, but we can do some things to help.

First, we must be informed. Who is hungry? Why are they hungry? What can we do about it? Second, we must pray. Prayer for world hunger is a mandate in today's world. Third, we need to change our life-style. We must ask ourselves some hard questions. How much can we have when others are hungry? How long can we live in luxury when people are starving all around us? We are rich Christians in a hungry world. What should be our response? We must grapple with these questions.

There are other strategies, however, which can be implemented immediately. Let me suggest two such steps. First, we can join others in the fight against hunger. I would encourage each of you to become a member of *Bread for the World*, a Christian organization which works through the political system to help hungry people. Second, we can give money to help relieve hunger. Please consider giving a substantial offering this year to world hunger efforts through the Home and Foreign Mission Board.

This money is given in Christ's name. It's not only used for relief, but it also helps people become self-sufficient in the area of food production.

Hungry People Were Fed (vv. 19b-21)

Let's review our story. First, a problem arose. Jesus and His disciples were surrounded by a hungry crowd. Second, a decision was made. Jesus said, "Give them something to eat." Third, a strategy was developed. Jesus devised a plan to feed the people. Finally, Jesus fed them in God's name. The problem was resolved. Hungry people were fed. Jesus blessed the food and, through a miracle of God, all were fed. And when we get informed, when we pray, when we change our life-style, when we join others such as *Bread for the World* in the fight against hunger, and when we give—hungry people will be fed once again. God will take our prayers, our dollars, and our concern, and He will multiply them on behalf of hungry people.

"Give them something to eat" said our Lord. What will be our response? What will be your response?

Another text which works well for a sermon on hunger is 1 John 3:17-18. A powerful sermon can be developed by simply walking through the passage.

"But If Any One Has the World's Goods" (v. 17a)

Who has the world's goods—we do! America is the richest country on the planet. We own houses, cars, furniture, clothes, savings accounts, pension plans, insurance, televisions, VCRs, video cameras, stereos, dishwashers, computers, and so forth. This verse is talking about us. Even middle-class Americans who earn a modest income are rich in comparison with the rest of the world. Our garbage disposals and cats eat better than one fourth of the world's population.

"And Sees His Brother in Need" (v. 17b)

Millions of our brothers and sisters are in awesome need. Several years ago, the *Arkansas Baptist Newsmagazine* reported, "This year, between 13 million and 18 million people will starve to death. That's 35,000 people a day or 24 people a minute. The number of people who die from hunger every 2 days equals the number who were killed instantly by the atom bomb in Hiroshima."

Our brother is in great need. The reasons are varied and complicated, but the need is simple—they are hungry.

"Yet Closes His Heart Against Him" (v. 17c)

It's easy to do this. We know people are hungry but we ignore the problem. We close our hearts against the hungry individually and corporately. It may be apathy which causes us to do this, or selfishness, or maybe even a sense of helplessness at the extent of the problem. But regardless of the reasons, we often close our hearts to hungry people.

"How Does God's Love Abide in Him?" (v. 17d)

This is a rhetorical question. John is saying that if we love like we ought, we won't close our hearts. Instead, we'll do all we can to help. This isn't just the message of 1 John, but of the entire Bible. We see it in the law. In Deuteronomy we read, "Open wide your hand, . . . to the needy"(15:11). The same theme can be found in the prophets. Isaiah said, "Pour yourself out for the hungry"(58:10). We also find this message in the Old Testament writings. In Proverbs we read, "He who is kind to the poor lends to the Lord, and he will repay him for his deed"(19:17). The New Testament proclaims the same message. We see it in the Gospels. In Matthew, Jesus says, "I was hungry and you gave me food."(25:35). The same message is found in the New Testament letters. In 2 Corinthians, Paul says, "As a matter of equity your abundance at this time should supply their want." James proclaimed, "If a brother or sister is ill-clad and in lack of daily food, and one of you says to them, 'Go in peace, be warmed and filled,' without giving them the things needed for the body, what does it profit? So faith by itself, if it has no works, is dead"(2:15-17). All of which brings us to verse 18 in our text.

"Little children, let us not love in word or speech but in deed and in truth." We are not to talk about our concern for the world's hungry. We must prove our concern with action and deeds.

(At this point in the sermon, suggest several things which can be done to help. See the previous sermon for specific suggestions.)

Another effective passage for World Hunger Day is the story of the rich man and Lazarus found in Luke 16:19-31. You could title your sermon, "Lazarus Revisited." You could revolve your sermon around three points: (1) Lazarus retold. Simply retell the story. You might want to read Clarence Jordan's version of this story from the *Cotton Patch Version of Luke and Acts.* (2) Lazarus relived. During this part of the sermon, point out that hunger is still a major problem, just as it was for Lazarus. (3) Lazarus waits our response. At this point in the sermon, challenge your congregation to do something about world hunger. Offer specific and concrete suggestions.

13

Senior Adult Day

Senior Adult Day provides an opportunity to affirm and encourage senior adults in the congregation. Senior adults are extremely important in the life of the church. As their numbers grow in our nation, their numbers will also grow in our churches. We must never neglect their significance and importance in God's kingdom.

I love senior adults. They were among my best supporters, encouragers, and friends when I was in the pastorate. I always enjoyed observing Senior Adult Day. With advance planning, Senior Adult Day can be a great day of worship in your church.

Worship Ideas

The key to a successful Senior Adult Day worship service is senior adult involvement. Senior adults should lead the entire service. Have seniors give the announcements, take up the offering, offer the prayers, fill the choir loft, sing solos, give testimonies, and lead responsive readings. You might even have a senior adult preach the sermon. In my last pastorate we had a retired pastor in our congregation. On one Senior Adult Day we asked him to preach the sermon. He did an excellent job. The order of worship we usually used for Senior Adult Day follows.

The Worship of God

It Is Good to Sing Praises to the Lord
(Ps. 92:1)

Prelude

Choral Call to Worship..................... Senior Adult Choir

Hymn .... To God Be the Glory .... No. 33

Invocation

To Declare God's Steadfast Love and Faithfulness
(Ps. 92:2)

> Leader: When I am old and gray-headed, O God, forsake me not;
> People: Until I have shown thy strength to this generation,
> Leader: And thy power to everyone that is to come.
> People: Gray hair is a crown of splendor,
> Leader: It is attained by a righteous life.
> People: They still bear fruit in old age, they will stay fresh and green.
> Leader: Even to your old age and gray hairs, I am God,
> People: I am He who will sustain you.
> Leader: I have made you and I will carry you;
> People: I will sustain you and I will rescue you.
> All: Gray hair is a crown of splendor. They still bear fruit in old age.

Hymn .... How Great Thou Art .... No. 35

Testimony

Solo .... All the Way My Savior Leads Me

Offertory Hymn .... Heavenly Sunlight .... No. 472

Offertory

They Still Bring Forth Fruit in Old Age
(Ps. 92:14)

Scripture Readings................ Genesis 12:1-7; Exodus 3:1-12

Anthem.......... Look and Live.......... Senior Adult Choir

Sermon .... No Retirement .... Pastor

Invitation Hymn ..... Take My Life, Lead Me, Lord...... No. 368

Benediction

Postlude

No Retirement

Ps. 92:14; Gen. 12:1-7; Ex. 3:1-12

In his book, *Strengthening Your Grip*, Charles Swindoll wrote about growing old. He said that you know you're getting old when . . .

 . . . most of your dreams are reruns,
 . . . the airline attendant offers you "coffee, tea, or Milk of Magnesia,"
 . . . you sit down in a rocking chair and you can't get it started,
 . . . your mind makes commitments your body can't keep,
 . . . the little gray-haired lady you help across the street is your wife!
 . . . reading *The Total Woman* makes you sleepy,
 . . . everything hurts, and what doesn't hurt doesn't work,
 . . . you sink your teeth into a juicy steak and they stay there,
 . . . you watch a pretty girl go by and your pacemaker makes the garage door open.[1]

Swindoll continues his humor on aging by sharing this poem about the senior adult years.

I get up each morning, dust off my wits,
Pick up the paper and read the obits.
If my name is missing, I know I'm not dead
So I eat a good breakfast—and go back to bed.[2]

While it's good to be able to laugh about growing old, some things about aging are not laughing matters. One which should concern us all are the myths some people have about senior adults. Ageism is a real problem in our country. Many younger people have false ideas about aging and about the elderly.

Several years ago Lou Harris conducted a poll among young people. The subject was aging. Harris learned that the younger generation had a portrait of senior adults as unalert, physically inert, narrow-minded, ineffective, sexually finished, old people rotting away in poor health, without proper medical care and without enough money to live on.

Countering this total myth, Harris said, "Society's view of older persons is a flat and unmitigated libel and downright lie." Senior adults are not a bunch of senile, physically incapacitated, depressed, old people wasting away in rocking chairs. Senior adults are very much alive and have much to offer. The senior years can be fruitful and exciting years. The senior years are not a time to retire from life and to withdraw from service. Rather, the Bible tells us that, "They still bring forth fruit in old age" (Ps. 92:14).

Although I am young, I love, respect, and appreciate senior adults. They are among the most dedicated and loyal persons in Christ's church. Senior adults are my friends, supporters, and advisers. I appreciate senior adults.

If time permitted I'd say many things to senior adults on this Senior Adult Day. I'd like to talk about your value and worth, about how much I appreciate you and your commitment, and many other affirmations. But the message I want to share today is short and simple. Senior adults—don't retire! Don't retire from life; you have too much left to live. And don't retire from serving God; you have too much left to offer in God's kingdom. You can retire from your career if you choose, but don't retire from service to the Lord.

Occasionally, when senior adults are asked to serve in the church, they sometimes say, "I've served my time." I've always hated that phrase, "I've served my time." It sounds like they have served several years in the state penitentiary! Nobody ever serves their time in the kingdom of God—not until they die. We may change some roles, but God expects us to serve Him all our life. Even a shut-in senior adult can serve God. He or she can be a prayer warrior and serve God and their church through continual prayer.

Jewish rabbis have known for centuries the value of senior adults. In the Talmud, a collection of Jewish teachings and sayings, the rabbis wrote: "He who learns from the young eats unripe grapes and drinks new wine. He who learns from the old eats ripe grapes and drinks old wine." The Jews have great appreciation for the wisdom and value of senior adults.

Don Moore, executive director of the Arkansas State Baptist Convention once said: "Senior adults have it all. They have the time, desire, ability and often the finances to do great things. This is not true of all senior adults, but it is of many . . . we need to give more time in harnessing the great potential of these people."

God affirms the value of older persons. God expects them to serve Him all their lives in whatever capacity they can. This is a clear biblical principle. God would say to senior adults today—don't retire from serving Me. You are still needed in My army; you are still a servant in My kingdom.

We see this message in many passages of Holy Scripture. In Psalm 92:14 the Bible says, "They will still bear fruit in old age, they will stay fresh and green, proclaiming; 'The Lord is upright, he is my Rock' "(NIV).

They will still bear fruit in old age! Senior adults still have much to offer. Senior adults are valuable. "Gray hair is a crown of splendor," says Proverbs 16:31(NIV). What do seniors have to offer?

Senior adults have wisdom. Job 12:12 says, "Is not wisdom found among the aged?"(NIV)

Seniors have a great testimony to share. Deuteronomy 32:7 says, "Remember the days of old; consider the generations long past; Ask your father and he will tell you, your elders, and they will explain to you"(NIV).

Senior adults have time. In most cases, seniors have more time to serve than younger persons who are still raising children and have full-time careers.

Seniors have money. Their gifts to God's work are extremely important. They have financial resources and are less selfish in sharing their resources. Many elderly church members put the rest of us to shame. I know many widows who, in spite of financial struggles, tithe their monthly Social Security check. Many of us who are younger give only our leftovers.

Senior adults are often spiritually mature. They have great insight and knowledge to share. We would do well to listen to them.

The Bible clearly teaches that senior adults are valuable to God and have much to offer in God's service. The Bible not only teaches that as a principle, it illustrates it in the lives of many people. Our Scripture readings today are vivid examples. The two most significant characters of the Old Testament are Abraham and Moses. And both of them were old men when they did their best work and service.

Think of Abraham. He was an old man when God called him and his wife to be the parents of the Jewish nation. They were old, but God used them in a mighty way. Listen to Frederick Buechner's humorous retelling of the old story.

> The place to start is with a woman laughing. She is an old woman, and, after a lifetime in the desert, her face is cracked and rutted like a six-month drought. She hunches her shoulders around her ears and starts to shake. She squinnies her eyes shut, and her laughter is all China teeth and wheeze and tears running down as she rocks back and forth in her kitchen chair. She is laughing because she is pushing ninety-one hard and has just been told she is going to have a baby. Even though it was an angel who told her, she can't control herself, and her husband can't control himself either. He keeps a straight face a few seconds longer than she does, but he ends by cracking up too.
>
> The old woman's name is Sarah of course and the old man's name is Abraham, and they are laughing at the idea of a baby's being born in the geriatric ward and medicare's picking up the tab. They are laughing because the angel not only seems to believe it but seems to expect them to believe it too. They are laughing because with part of themselves they do believe it. They are laughing because with another part of themselves they know it would take a fool to believe it.[3]

And yet, God took this elderly couple and blessed the world through them. The Savior of the world, Jesus Christ our Lord, came from the Jewish nation whom Abraham and Sarah began.

Or consider Moses. Moses was eighty when God called him to set the Jewish people free. Moses is the greatest figure in the Old Testament. The Ten Commandments came through Moses. Yet, he made his greatest accomplishments in the last third of his life. At a time when we would be enjoying retirement and collecting our pension checks, Moses was leading the people of God out of bondage in Egypt to the promised land.

God can and does use senior adults in His service. Seniors have great value, worth, and potential. And so on this senior adult day, I have a simple message for our senior adults. Don't retire! Keep on living life to the fullest and keep on serving God. Remember what the Bible says, "They will still bear fruit in old age, they will stay fresh and green, proclaiming, 'The Lord is upright; he is my Rock.' "

Notes

1. Chuck Swindoll, *Strengthening Your Grip* (Waco, Tex.: Word Books, n.d.).
2. Ibid.
3. Frederick Buechner, *Telling the Truth: The Gospel as Tragedy, Comedy, and Fairy Tale* (New York: Harper and Row, 1977).

14

World Peace Day

Many denominations have designated one Sunday per year as world peace day. In my denomination this special emphasis is called "Day of Prayer for World Peace." In a world embroiled in conflict and violence, God calls His people to be peacemakers. It is appropriate, therefore, that this theme be highlighted in worship.

Worship Ideas

The Worship of God

Blessed Be the Lord God of Israel (Luke 1:68)

Concerns of the Church
Prelude
Call to Worship
    Leader: Blessed be the Lord God of Israel,
    People: For he has visited and redeemed his people,
    Leader: and has raised up a horn of salvation for us
    People: in the house of his servant David.
Hymn . . . . Praise to the Lord, the Almighty. . . . . No. 10
Invocation
Hymn . . . . This Is My Father's World . . . . No. 155
Discipline of Silence
Doxology
Offertory Prayer
Offering

Guide Our Feet into the Way of Peace (Luke 1:79)

Scripture Readings
Prayer for Peace

> Dear Lord,
> We live in a world of war and rumors of war. Forgive us Lord for the part we play in contributing to this lack of peace. We pray for inner peace within our own hearts and minds. We pray for peace in our relationships with others. We pray for peace between nations throughout the world. Help us to obey Your command to seek peace and be peacemakers. We pray these things in the name of Jesus Christ our Lord, the Prince of Peace. Amen.

Anthem.......... Peace in Our Time, O Lord .... Choir
Sermon .... Blessed Are the Peacemakers .... Pastor
Hymn of Invitation ..... Peace in Our Time, O Lord...... No. 310
Benediction
Postlude

Scripture Readings

Consider enlisting several laypeople to lead the Scripture reading. When I led this service in my church, I asked five laypeople to participate. Rather than come to the pulpit, each person stood at their pew and read their passages one after another. The texts were: Isaiah 2:4; Psalm 34:14; Hebrews 12:14; Romans 14:19; Matthew 5:9.

Involving Children

Another possibility is to ask a children's Sunday School class (the week before World Peace Day) to write a short paper, "Why I Want World Peace." Have several of them read their papers on World Peace Day. Another option would be to have their Sunday School teacher read them.

Testimonies

Consider having people share testimonies on "Peace with God," "Peace with Others," and "Peace Between Nations." It would add to the service if someone from another country could share the testimony on peace between nations. Sermons on these subjects would also be appropriate for this special Sunday.

Blessed Are the Peacemakers
Matt. 5:9

Several years ago a friend and I engaged in a lively conversation concerning the growing peace movement throughout the world. I soon learned that my friend was no friend of this movement. Near the end of our discussion he said, "The people involved in the peace movement are all a bunch of clowns."

Clowns . . . I wonder about that. It reminds me of an old story told by Soren Kierkegaard. In this story, a circus tent catches fire. The first person who noticed the fire was a clown. In the panic of the moment he ran into the ring and began screaming, "Everyone must leave immediately. The tent is on fire!"

The clown continued his desperate warning but the people, knowing that clowns will be clowns, howled with laughter as the tent began to burn around them.

Many people today are warning us that the tent is on fire. They are concerned about the growing stockpile of nuclear weapons and warring nations. These people are not clowns. They include housewives, preachers, doctors, nuclear physicists, and even military leaders. They warn us that the world tent really is on fire and unless we do something to escape the situation, we're all going to burn—literally.

Today is set apart by our denomination as Day of Prayer for World Peace. It is a day to reflect on war and peace and our Christian responsibility to be peacemakers. Although people have different opinions about how to seek peace, we must involve ourselves in the quest for peace.

The Problem

We live in an increasingly dangerous world. The threat of war and especially nuclear war is awesome and real. An organization of nuclear scientists puts out a bulletin. In the bulletin is a clock called the doomsday clock. Periodically, they set the clock forward or backward to reflect their view on the nearness of nuclear war. The time of nuclear war is midnight. At times, the clock stands just moments away from midnight.

These scientists believe that nuclear war is probable. They are not alone. A survey once showed that most Americans believe that the U.S. will be involved in nuclear war. Way back in 1982 the Joint Chiefs of Staff predicted a fifty/fifty chance of nuclear war by 1985. Thankfully, that did not happen. But it illustrates the threat.

The United States and the Soviet Union have a tremendous nuclear arsenal. Nuclear weapons continue to get more sophisticated and more deadly. Other nations are getting their hands on these weapons. In spite of sweeping changes in many communist countries, the threat of nuclear weapons is still great.

The danger of nuclear war by accident is also a problem. In an eighteen-month period several years ago, the U.S. nuclear warning system had 151 false alarms.

War, in general, and especially nuclear war, threatens everything we hold dear. Many of us have seen movies depicting the results of nuclear war such as *The Day After*. These movies portray a horrible picture of what nuclear war could be like. Since *The Day After* was released almost a decade ago, many nuclear experts criticized the movie as not being realistic. They say that a real nuclear war would be much worse than movies portray.

The cost and threat of nuclear weapons are horrifying. Many believe that a nuclear war would destroy the environment so badly that it could not recover. The Sierra Club, the largest environmental group in the country, calls the nuclear arms race *the* major environmental issue. We just sang, "This Is My Father's World." We now have the ability to destroy His world.

Nuclear weapons threaten more than the planet. Our economy is damaged by preparation for war. Many experts are now saying that we cannot afford to continue the arms race. The cost is so expensive that it could eventually collapse the economy.

The situation threatens our psychological well-being as well. Several years ago, a poll was taken of thousands of teenagers. Many expected to be killed by nuclear weapons rather than die of old age. Such fears can cause serious emotional damage.

War and the preparation for war also threatens our ability to help needy people. President Dwight Eisenhower once said, "Every gun that is made, every warship launched, every rocket fired, signifies in the final sense, a theft from those who are hungry and are not fed, those who are cold and are not clothed."

In recent years, I have read accounts of people who survived the atomic bombs dropped on Japan during World War II. To read such reports is frightening and nauseating. If I were to read some of those reports it would make you sick. And today's nuclear weapons are even more powerful than the ones dropped on Japan. It's been estimated that the United States and the Soviet Union have enough nuclear weapons to kill every man, woman, boy, and girl on the planet twelve times over again. When will it be enough?

Someone once said that nuclear war is the ultimate profanity. We live in a dangerous world. The problem is real and frightening.

The Bible

As Christians, when we face a problem, we must turn to God's Word for direction. The Bible has much to say about war and peace. The Bible teaches us that war and conflict are the result of sin. God, however, wants peace for His creation. The Scriptures are full of this truth.

Psalm 34:14 says, "Seek peace, and pursue it." Isaiah 31:1 warns us not to trust in chariots, horses, and weapons of war, but to trust God. In Isaiah 2:4 we read God's ideal for His creation, "They shall beat their swords into plowshares, and their spears into pruning hooks; nation shall not lift up sword against nation, neither shall they learn war any more."

The New Testament is also full of passages which illustrate God's desire for peace and not war. In Luke 19:42 Jesus weeps over Jerusalem and says, "Would that even today you knew the things that make for peace!" Hebrews 12:14 urges, "Strive for peace with all men." Romans 14:19 says, "Let us then pursue what makes for peace." In 1 Corinthians 7:15 Paul wrote, "God has called us to peace." In Luke 1:79 Zechariah proclaimed that Christ would "guide our feet into the way of peace." Jesus tells us in Matthew 5:9, "Blessed are the peacemakers, for they shall be called sons of God."

God knows the evils of war. God wants peace. And more than that, God wants His children to be peacemakers. Peacemaking is not an optional endeavor for the Christian. God requires us to seek peace in our world.

What Can We Do?

This question sparks controversy among good Christian people. On the one hand is the pacifist who thinks all war and weapons are sin and refuses to engage in war. On the other hand you have people who think that the only way to prevent war is to have tremendous military power. Honest differences exist between Christians concerning seeking peace. Regardless of our differences, there is some common ground.

First, nobody wants a war. The stakes are too high. One U.S. president said that a nuclear war cannot be won and must never be fought. In the popular movie *War Games* this reality is voiced by a computer. Speaking about nuclear war as a game, the computer said, "The only way to win is not to play." Second, almost everyone believes we must have deterrence. With the exception of a few pacifists, most Christians agree that in our broken world, a strong military is necessary. Third, most people want arms control if it can be verifiable. So, in spite of our differences, there is some common ground. We can begin at these points of agreement and then move toward some solutions.

More specifically, what can individual Christians do to help this problem? How can we be peacemakers in today's world? Let me suggest three concrete steps that you and I can take.

First, we need to be informed. In Hosea 4:6 the prophet said that his people were destroyed by lack of knowledge. Christian people must become informed about war, peace, and nuclear weapons. The situation is too grave and the stakes are too high to be uninformed or disinterested.

Second, we can become involved. Christians must insist that our national leaders work for an end to the arms race and work for peace and not war. We need to vote for persons who will obey the biblical command to seek peace and be peacemakers. We need to write our leaders and tell them that we expect them to seek peace.

Third, we can pray. That's the primary purpose of this special day— Day of Prayer for World Peace. We believe in prayer. We pray for missions, the sick, the hungry, those in grief, the lost, and for other needs. Anything we care about, we pray about. Someone once asked Thomas Merton, a Catholic monk, how he could spend his life shut away in a monastery when there was so much suffering in the world and so much needed to be done. Merton responded by saying, "The difference between you and me, my friend, is that I believe in prayer."

Pray for world peace. Several results will occur. First, it will focus your attention on this serious problem. Second, prayer moves us to action. If we pray about world peace we'll be likely to do something about it. Third, prayer changes things. God is still alive and powerful and the prayers of His people have an impact on world peace.

We live in a dangerous world. God's Word on this subject is clear. He wants peace and He expects His people to be peacemakers. A starting place would be to become informed, get involved, and pray. "Blessed are the peacemakers," said Jesus, "for they shall be called sons of God."

15

Men's Day

Several denominations observe an annual men's day. My denomination calls it "Baptist Men's Day." It provides an opportunity to affirm the men of the church and challenge them to greater service.

When I served as a pastor, my church observed Men's Day every year with a lay service. It soon became a highlight of our year. I did not preach a sermon on Men's Day. Rather, I asked several of our men to give testimonies, read Scripture passages, and lead worship in other ways. We also had a men's choir and men's quartet. We always began the day with a men's breakfast.

Since there is no sermon on Men's Day, I'll simply share a suggested order of worship. This one is developed from the hymn, "Rise Up, O Men of God."

The Worship of God

Rise Up, O Men of God

Prelude
Call to Worship . . . . . . Rise Up, O Men of God . . . . . . Men's Choir
Invocation
Introduction to Men's Day . . . . Pastor
Hymn . . . . Blessed Assurance . . . . No. 334

Have Done with Lesser Things

Scripture Reading
Testimony

Hymn . . . . Heaven Came Down . . . . No. 425
Scripture Reading
Testimony

Give Heart and Mind and Soul and Strength

Choral Anthem . . . . . . Standing on the Promises . . . . . . Men's Choir
Testimony
Hymn . . . . Love Lifted Me . . . . No. 462
Offertory Prayer
Offering

To Serve the King of Kings

Men's Quartet . . . . Amazing Grace
Concluding Remarks . . . . Pastor
Hymn of Invitation . . . . No. 191
   I Have Decided to Follow Jesus
Choral Benediction . . . . Men's Choir
Postlude

Part IV
Special Sundays from the
Local Church Calendar

16

Deacon Ordination

Ordaining a new deacon is a special time in the life of the deacon and the church. Careful planning can result in a significant worship service for all involved.

Two options exist for observing deacon ordination. You can focus the entire service around the ordination, or ordination can be one portion of a regular worship service. If the worship service and sermon are on a theme which fits the occasion, such as service or commitment, it's possible to have a meaningful ordination as a part of a larger service. Although I've done it both ways, I prefer focusing the entire service around the ordination.

Worship Ideas

The Worship of God

We Gather for Worship

Prelude
Responsive Reading.................................... No. 522
Hymn 35............. How Great Thou Art............. No. 35
Invocation
Hymn 411........ Serve the Lord with Gladness........ No. 411

We Prepare for Ordination

Scripture Readings
      Old Testament Lesson..................... Exodus 18:13-24

New Testament Lesson . . . . 1 Timothy 3:8-13
Sermon . . . . Partners in Ministry . . . . Pastor
Solo . . . . Make Me a Servant

We Ordain Our New Deacons

Introduction to Ordination
Testimonies
Charge to the Deacons
Laying on of Hands
Charge to the Church
Prayer of Dedication
Presentation of Certificates and Gifts

We Surrender to God's Service

Hymn . . . . Stand Up, Stand Up for Jesus . . . . No. 391
Benediction
Hand of Fellowship by the Congregation

Involvement of Deacons

Involve as many deacons as possible in this service. Ask the deacons of your church to lead prayers, read Scripture, give the charges, and so forth. If one of your deacon candidates has an ordained relative, consider asking them to participate in the service.

Testimonies

Having the deacon candidates share a brief testimony adds much to the service. If you are ordaining a large number of deacons and it would take too long for all of them to share their testimonies, consider asking a few.

Laying On of Hands

The laying on of hands is the most moving part of the ordination service. In many cases, only ordained persons are asked to participate. A growing number of churches, however, are inviting the entire congregation to lay on hands. This is in line with the biblical account; it allows the entire congregation to participate in this special setting apart for ministry. If your congregation is large and would take an inordinate amount of time to do this, consider asking representatives (mission leaders, Sunday School director, choir representatives, program leaders, and so forth) to participate.

Another idea for enhancing this part of the service is to invite the spouses of the deacon candidates to stand or kneel beside or behind them during the laying on of hands. This symbolizes the spouse's support during this important time of dedication.

Charge to the Deacons

The new deacons should be challenged to make a public commitment to deacon ministry. A possible charge follows. "Do you promise to strive to live in such a way as to bring honor to Christ and His church, and do you promise, in the presence of this congregation, to accept the responsibility of the office of deacon, and to the best of your knowledge and ability, to carry out the duties of this office? If so, please say 'I do.' "

Charge to the Church

The church should be charged with supporting the ministry of the new deacons. A possible charge follows. "Do you acknowledge these persons as deacons in our church, do you promise to encourage and pray for them in this office and to cooperate with them in the fulfillment of the mission of the church? If so, will you please say 'I do' ?"

Certificate and Gift

A certificate of ordination and an appropriate gift (a Bible or book on deacon ministry, and so forth) would be appreciated by the deacon.

Fellowship

A deacon-sponsored fellowship or meal after the ordination service adds a positive dimension to the ordination service. If the ordination is held in the morning, consider a potluck luncheon for the whole congregation. If that is not desirable, consider having a deacons-only luncheon.

Partners in Ministry
Exodus 18:13-24

(Note: Due to the extra worship activities during this service, the sermon should be brief.)

I saw a cartoon the other day featuring a deacon and his pastor. The deacon said, "Pastor, I have some good news and some bad news. The good news is that the deacons have purchased you a retirement home. The bad news is that you move in tomorrow."

A long-standing tradition exists of pastor/deacon jokes. Go to any pastors' conference and you're bound to hear one. Usually, however, they are told in jest. Although conflict exists between some deacon bodies and their pastor, in most churches the pastor/deacon relationship is healthy.

As I understand it, deacons and pastors are called by God to be partners in ministry. That's the principle behind today's text. In this story, Moses was trying to solve all the problems among the people of Israel. But as we read in our text, it wasn't working too well. It wasn't good for Moses nor for the people.

Moses' father-in-law suggested that Moses get some help. He advised Moses to delegate some responsibility to others. He realized that if Moses tried to do it all by himself, he would completely burn out and the people's needs would go unmet. Moses gave heed to this advice and selected able leaders to help him in his task.

What was true for Moses is true of every pastor. No pastor can do all the work of the church by himself. Alone no pastor can lead the church, proclaim the gospel, and care for all the church membership. It's an impossible task, even in small churches. Like Moses of old, modern-day pastors need help for the task.

In reality, the entire church must be involved in carrying out the mission of the church. Every member must carry his or her weight. If God's work is to be accomplished, all must participate.

But pastors also need special helpers. They need partners in ministry. This is the role of deacons. Deacons are not financial advisers or business leaders or authority figures. Their job isn't to keep the pastor in line.

Rather, deacons are called to be partners in ministry with their pastor. They are called to be servants of God, with the pastor, for the people.

Pastors and deacons are part of the pastoral ministries team in the local church. They are to work together to proclaim the gospel to believers and unbelievers, to lead the church to accomplish its mission, and to care for the needs of people.

This church needs that kind of deacon. This pastor needs that kind of deacon. Nobody, not even Moses himself, can do all that needs to be done among God's people. Pastors need partners in ministry, and that is what deacons are called to be—servants of God, with the pastor, for the people.

17

Stewardship Sunday

When I first entered the pastorate, I was hesitant to talk about money. In time, however, that changed. As I studied the Bible in more detail, I realized that Holy Scripture constantly talks about money. God knows that we are economic creatures. He cares deeply about how we earn and spend our income. Moreover, the church depends on money to do God's work.

It is appropriate, therefore, to address the subject of giving in our worship and preaching. Although it can be overdone, it's important to occasionally speak about giving. Like many pastors, I preached on stewardship at least once per year during our stewardship campaign. A possible order of worship and sermon follow.

The Worship of God

An Offering of Praise

Prelude
Call to Worship . . . Now Let Us All Praise God and Sing . . . . Choir
Responsive Reading. . . . . No. 521
The Greeting
Hymn . . . . O Worship the King. . . . . No. 30
Invocation

An Offering of Prayer

Hymn . . . . Sweet Hour of Prayer. . . . . No. 401
Discipline of Silence

Pastoral Prayer
The Lord's Prayer

An Offering of Possessions

Hymn . . . . Come, All Christians, Be Committed . . . . No. 362
Offertory Prayer
Offering

An Offering of Proclamation

Scripture Reading . . . . 1 Corinthians 16:1-2
Anthem
Sermon . . . . Concerning the Collection
Invitation Hymn . . . . . . Take My Life, and Let It Be . . . . . . No. 373
Benediction
Postlude

Concerning the Collection
1 Cor. 16:1-2

A mother once had a son who did not like neckties. In fact, he hated them. His mother, however, thought he should wear them. So on his birthday, she gave him two beautiful silk ties. Upon her departure he promptly put them into his closet with the many other unused ties he had accumulated.

This son, however, was considerate to his mother. On his next visit home, out of respect for his mother, he decided to wear one of the new ties she gave him for his birthday. When he walked in the door, his mother looked at his tie and said, "What's wrong with the other one?"

Well, you can only wear one tie at a time. And a preacher can only preach on one subject at a time. Today that subject is money. I'm going to talk about financial support of Christ's church. I have other ties in the closet—other messages to preach. But today I want to bring out the stewardship message and discuss it with you.

I used to pride myself on never preaching about money. I've been convicted, however, to speak about it more often. Money is a major subject in the Bible. Jesus spoke more about money than He did heaven. Money is important to us, it's important to God, and it's important to the life of our church. So, I've decided to preach on it at least once per year—whether we need it or not! And since we are in the middle of our stewardship campaign, it's an appropriate time to broach the subject.

In today's text, Paul speaks about the collection. He offers practical guidance about giving. Let's look closely at what he said.

The Period of the Collection

In this passage, Paul told the Christians in Corinth to give "on the first day of every week." In other words, we are to give regularly and systematically.

God tells us here and in other places in the Bible to give to His work on a regular basis. Consistent giving is God's command. This means we are to give even when we are on vacation and even when we have other things we would like to buy. We are to give even when it's inconvenient.

A few years ago, I went to the hospital to visit a woman named Sue Williams, a dedicated member of the church I pastored. Sadly, Sue was dying of cancer and this was one of the last times I ever saw her alive. We had a special visit and prayer together that day. As I prepared to leave she said, "Brother Martin, please hand me my purse." After I handed it to her, she got out her checkbook and wrote a check for that month's tithe.

Sue was not a wealthy woman. She was struggling with major medical bills. She was near death. Yet, it was important to her to give and give regularly—even when she was in the hospital. God wants us to give to His work on a regular basis.

The People of the Collection

Notice what Paul wrote here, "On the first day of every week, *each of you* (author's italics) is to put something aside." Paul said that everyone is to give something. All are responsible to fund God's work in the world.

In most American churches, 20 percent of the people give 80 percent of the money. Thirty percent of the people give 20 percent of the money. And 50 percent give absolutely nothing at all. This should not be! All of us are commanded to give to God's work.

The Place of the Collection

In this passage, Paul told the people where to give their money. They were to give it to the church. The first day of the week is the day to come to church and worship. The people were to bring their gifts to the storehouse—the church.

Many good Christian organizations want our money. But our first priority must always be the local church. This is God's plan and God's command. It's also a good investment.

Several years ago I decided to purchase a home computer. I sought the advice of a friend who was a computer expert. His advice was, "Make sure to get the biggest bang for your buck."

When we give to God's work through the local church, we get the biggest bang for our religious buck. Other Christian causes compete for our money, but none should take priority over the local church. There's no question that the local church is the most effective expenditure of our limited gifts to God's work.

Several years ago, a study compared the seven leading television ministries to the Southern Baptist Convention's Cooperative Program. The results were recorded in the April 6, 1987 issue of *U.S. News and World Report*. The annual income of those television ministries was 293 million dollars. These ministries supported four churches, one hospital, five colleges, and seven weekly television programs.

During that same year, the Southern Baptist Convention Cooperative Program gifts totaled 231 million dollars, 60 million less than the seven television ministries. This money, however, supported 3,450 foreign missionaries, 3,792 home missionaries, 438 chaplains, 67 colleges, 1,100 student ministers, thirty-two weekly broadcast programs, and spent over five million dollars for world hunger.

There is absolutely no comparison! Giving to your local church gives you "the biggest bang for your buck." When we give, we must give to the right place. That place is the local church.

The Portion of the Collection

Paul explained in this passage that each is to give "as he may prosper." God isn't concerned about the amount we give but the percentage we give. Widows who tithe their Social Security check give a far larger portion of their income than wealthy people who give thousands, yet give only a small percentage of their income.

God's Word teaches us to tithe. That should be our goal. If we can't tithe today, we should be moving in that direction.

Why should we give a portion of our income to the local church? Some people say we should give in order to gain. I've heard testimonies about how people tithed their way to being a millionaire. Perhaps that's true for some people. My experience has been different. I've discovered that when I tithe, I have 10 percent less money to spend! I give that portion, however, because I love God and God's church. It's a matter of commitment. We are called and commanded to give our portion.

The Purpose of the Collection

This particular collection was collected for needy people in Jerusalem. The purpose of our giving is to meet needs—spiritual and physical. We give to share the gospel and to support God's work locally and around the globe. No organization has a greater purpose than God's church. And God funds His church through the giving of His people.

What does the Bible teach us about giving? This passage makes it very clear. We are to give regularly. All of us are to give. We are to give to the local church. We are to give our portion. And we are to give for a great purpose—to support God's work. Will we do it?

Other Preaching Ideas

Numerous passages lend themselves to preaching about stewardship. Consider the following two texts.

Luke 21:1-4 is an excellent passage for a stewardship sermon. Consider preaching a simple sermon about the widow who gave two copper coins. Three points could be made. First, she gave. Considering that 50 percent of our church members don't give, this is a significant point. Second, she gave to the right place. She gave her money to support the temple—just as we should give to support the local church. Third, she gave sacrificially. She gave all she had.

Another possible passage is 2 Corinthians 8:1-5. In this passage, we have a wonderful example to follow in our giving. Careful study of the text shows that the churches of Macedonia gave sacrificially, joyfully, generously, voluntarily, and eagerly. They are our model. We should strive to follow their example.

18

Graduation

High-school graduation can be a special time in the life of the church. When I first entered the pastorate, I struggled with how to observe graduation. After all, it only involved a few people. I felt uneasy devoting an entire service to this theme. I've learned, however, that graduation is significant for the entire church. Elderly church members, for example, have watched these young people grow and develop since they played in the nursery. It thrills senior adults to see young people take this important step in life. Such a service can also be meaningful to the youth group and their parents. Everyone in the church, regardless of age, enjoys celebrating this important transition of life. Graduation offers an opportunity for the church family to experience meaningful worship.

Worship Ideas

Involve the seniors in every way possible during this service. You could also invite the entire youth group to participate. Consider having the graduating seniors and others in the youth group take up the offering, lead prayers, give testimonies, perform a skit, read Scripture, and sing. Have a special prayer for the graduating seniors and their families. Ask each senior and his or her parents to come forward for this prayer. This would be a good Sunday to ask the youth choir to sing. A gift for each graduating senior is in order. Many churches give a Bible or book. In one church I served, we gave the seniors a subscription to *The Student* magazine.

I attend a small church in Nashville. Last year we only had two graduating seniors. We decided, however, to go ahead and have a special graduation worship service. It proved to be one of the most moving services of the year.

During the service, both of our seniors and their families came to the front of the sanctuary. The parents briefly shared a few memories from their child's early years. Brothers and sisters of the two seniors shared some "sibling advice" for their graduating brother or sister. Then both seniors spoke to the congregation. They thanked the church for its role in their development. They recalled several specific people and events which impacted their life.

After the parents, siblings, and seniors spoke (each spoke for only a few moments), we had a video presentation of slides and music. About ten or fifteen slides of each senior was presented. The slides began with a baby picture and ended with their graduation picture.

After the youth choir sang the special music, our pastor preached a brief sermon. We concluded the service by making a circle around the sanctuary and singing "Friends."

This was the most moving graduation service I've ever attended. Both laughter and tears were abundant. And it was truly a worship experience. We thanked God for these young people and prayed for their future. We celebrated a major life transition and allowed God's presence to be an important part of that transition. We affirmed the significance of church involvement in the life of young people and their families. The service spoke to everyone in the congregation, not just the seniors and their families. Perhaps you can adapt some of the above ideas into a graduation service for your church. An order of worship follows.

The Worship of God

A Time of Praise

Prelude
Call to Worship . . . . Youth Choir
Hymn of Praise
Invocation (by a graduating senior or youth group member)

The Greeting
Doxology
Offering (Taken by seniors or youth group)

A Time of Recognition

Special Music (by one or more seniors or youth members)
Memories (parents of graduating seniors)
A word of advice (siblings of graduating seniors)
Testimonies (graduating seniors)
Video presentation

A Time of Proclamation

Scripture Reading
Special Music .... Youth Choir
Sermon
Invitation
Benediction (Congregation joins hands and sings "Friends")
Postlude

Sermon Suggestions

Numerous passages are appropriate for a graduation service. Consider preaching graduation sermons from Joshua 22:1-6, selected verses from Deuteronomy 4 (vv. 37-39 speaks about remembering your heritage, v. 40 speaks about keeping God's laws, v. 16 warns about making false gods, and so forth), and 1 Timothy 4:12. An entire sermon based on Mark 10:17-22 follows. It could be used during a morning worship service or as a baccalaureate sermon.

The Man Who Had Everything . . . Almost
(Mark 10:17-22)

I thought about our graduating seniors last week as I listened to the "Sesame Street Fairy Tale Album" with my three-year-old daughter. On this album Ernie tells a story about two brothers who always complained.

The story is about Ned and Ted—two brothers who lived quite well, yet constantly complained. They wished for a nicer house and more things. *If only they had more*, they thought, *they would be happy*. Then one day a fairy arrived. She said she would grant three wishes to them— one for Ned, one for Ted, and one that they both agreed on. Well, they stayed up all night arguing about what they should wish for. Ned wanted a ranch house, Ted wanted an old-fashioned place, and so on. They couldn't agree on anything. Finally, morning arrived. Ned was terribly hungry and, without thinking, said, "I wish I had a bowl of oatmeal to eat." And suddenly, a bowl of oatmeal appeared. Ted was furious. "I can't believe you wasted a whole wish on a stupid bowl of oatmeal. I wish that bowl of oatmeal would stick to your head." Then, suddenly, the bowl of oatmeal stuck to Ned's head. Two of their three wishes had now been wasted. For hours, Ned and Ted tried to get the bowl off of Ned's head. But it wouldn't budge. Finally, they had to decide on their third wish. Ned said, "I won't wish for anything except to get this bowl of oatmeal off my head." "We can't waste our last wish on that" said Ted, but in the end, he knew Ned would not wish for anything else. So the fairy returned and they used their last wish to remove the bowl of oatmeal from Ned's head.

Making Wishes

It's a time for that. Graduation is a time to make wishes about the future—a time to dream dreams. And I hope you won't waste your wishes and dreams like Ted and Ned did.

What is your wish for your future? Last fall, a research firm conducted a study of entering freshmen college students. They discovered that young people's greatest wish and ambition was to get a good job and make a lot of money.

The trouble is, making a lot of money and being successful by the world's standards isn't as satisfying as it looks. And that brings me to the passage of Scripture we read a moment ago. Our text tells about a young man who had it all. He was rich, he was young, and he was a ruler. You couldn't ask for much more.

Although he was rich, young, and powerful, he wasn't satisfied. He came to Jesus and asked what he must do to have everlasting life. And everlasting life isn't just life after death, it's also life here and now— meaningful life, life which satisfies. It's funny isn't it?—this young man had it all—but he didn't have a meaningful life. And that's a common experience. Many people have riches and fame and status—but are absolutely miserable.

This young man was searching for meaning in life. We all participate in this search. You're getting ready to search for many things—a vocation, a spouse, your own values and identity. But you will also be seeking a life which has meaning and purpose—a life which brings satisfaction and happiness and fulfillment.

Jesus' response to this rich young ruler contains a formula for finding a meaningful life. Jesus said three things to this man: (1) sell all that you have, (2) give it to the poor, and (3) come follow Me. Let's explore these statements for a few minutes.

Sell What You Have

Jesus rejects materialism as a way to find meaning. He tells this rich young ruler that he won't find what he's looking for in money and things. Jesus begins, therefore, by telling us that the path of materialism, popular as it is, is the wrong path for finding meaning.

Money and material things will never satisfy the deep longing of our heart for a meaningful life. Someone once asked a rich man, "How much money would it take to really be satisfied?" The rich man responded, "Just a little bit more." Money is like that. No matter how much we get, we always want more. Satisfaction and happiness remain elusive. We cannot find happiness through a higher standard of living. Jesus warns us that the path of materialism is a wrong path. Ultimately, it won't bring happiness, it won't give meaning to our lives. Money and things are not the answer.

But that's hard to believe, isn't it? We live in a culture which constantly bombards us with the message that the good life is found in money and things—in bigger and better—in corporate acquisition, luxurious houses, cars, and stock portfolios.

Young people, don't believe the lie that money and things are the most important thing in life. Jesus says that isn't the way to find meaning. In the end, a life consumed with making more and more money is a bankrupt life-style.

Jesus begins, therefore, by telling us a wrong path to find meaning. He now tells us the right paths.

Give it to the Poor

Jesus tells this man that one finds meaning in life through service to others. Give to the poor, care about others.

The Talmud (a Jewish collection of teachings) says a person should do three things in the course of life: have a child, plant a tree, and write a book. All of these represent ways in which we invest our life into the future and into others—a life of service to the world.

The people who are truly happy are those who know how to be a servant. Jesus said we find our life by losing it for others. When we stop spinning around ourselves and start caring about others—that's when we find meaning and happiness.

Young People—this world has so many needs. Millions are hurting. And you are venturing into that world. I plead with you not to waste your life on selfish pursuits but to invest your energies into serving others. That's the only way you'll ever be happy.

The German poet Goethe spent his whole life writing his masterpiece, *Faust.* He intended it to be his major statement about the meaning of life. He began writing the play at age twenty, then set it aside for other projects. He came back to it at age forty and completed it shortly before his death at age eighty-three.

At the onset of the play, Faust is pictured as a man who wants to experience everything, to live without limits. He wants to read all the books, speak all the languages, taste all the pleasures. So the devil gives him everything—wealth, political power, the ability to travel anywhere, and to be loved by any woman he desires. Faust has it all, but still he's not happy. However much wealth he acquires, however many women he seduces, there is an unsatisfied hunger within him.

By the end of the play Faust is an old man. Instead of winning fights and attracting young women, Faust is now at work building dikes to reclaim land from the sea for people to live and work on. He is investing his life in service for others. Now for the first time Faust can say, "Let this moment linger, it is so good."[1]

The German poet learned what Jesus said so long ago—that one finds meaning in life by being a servant—by caring about and serving humanity.

So far, Jesus tells us a wrong path to find meaning—the path of materialism, "Go sell what you have." And Jesus points to a right path—a life of service, "Give to the poor." There is a final word, however, in this formula of meaning.

Come, Follow Me

Finally, Jesus invites the rich young ruler to discipleship. Service alone isn't enough. Ultimate meaning is found only in spiritual dimensions. Jesus says the way to find true meaning is through serious commitment and discipleship.

All persons need to invest their lives in something bigger than themselves. A young man who ran away from his conventional middle-class home to join the Unification Church was asked why he had done it. He replied, "My father only talks about getting into college and getting a good job. Reverend Moon talks to me about helping him save the world."[2]

Reverend Moon does not offer ultimate meaning—but Jesus Christ does. If you want a life full of purpose and meaning then you need to be a disciple. You need to take Jesus up on His call: "Come, follow Me." That's where you'll find the life you're looking for. And one of the ways you can be a disciple is through active involvement in a church. So I urge you, as you leave home and venture out on your own, don't forget your spiritual roots—don't neglect involvement in church.

I began today's sermon by talking about wishes and dreams. I hope that as you make wishes for your future and as you dream dreams of what is to come, you'll reflect on what Jesus said in this passage of Scripture.

In the days ahead you'll hear from many sources that making lots of money and being successful is the way to meaningful life. Remember, however, what Jesus says. If money and success become ultimate for you, you are involved in a bankrupt and worthless pursuit. Things will never satisfy.

How can you find meaning as you leave this place and go on with your life? Jesus makes it clear—by service and discipleship. And now you must choose. You are adults now, venturing into an adult world. You must decide what your values are. You must choose whether you will be a servant and a disciple, or whether you'll live a self-centered life. It's your choice. Nobody can make it for you.

A story is told of an eccentric millionaire who once gathered all his friends together at his house. He took them out to his pool which was full of sharks. He told his guests, "the first one among you who will dive into the pool and swim across to the other side will get a million dollars." For a long while nobody said a word or made a move. Finally, someone splashed into the pool and swam to the other side. The sharks were closing in but just in the nick of time, the swimmer made it safely to the other side. To the rich man's surprise, it was his butler. "James," said the millionaire, "come into the house and I'll write you a check for a million dollars." "That's fine," said James, "but first I want to get the guy who pushed me into the pool!"

God won't make you follow His formula for finding meaning in life. He won't push you into a life of service and discipleship. You must decide for yourself. My hope and prayer is that you'll hear Jesus' warning not to seek meaning in materialism—and that you will hear His call to be a servant and a disciple, and that you will say yes.

Notes

1. Harold Kushner, *When All You've Ever Wanted Isn't Enough: the Search for a Life that Matters* (New York: Pocket Books, 1986), 47-48.
2. Ibid., 178.

19

Loyalty Day

Several years ago, the church I pastored needed a shot in the arm. We were in a slump. Attendance and giving were down and there seemed to be a status-quo, mediocre spirit among us. Several of my pastor friends had experimented with a "Loyalty Day" in their church. Each one reported a successful Loyalty Day. I figured it couldn't hurt and might help so we scheduled it on the calendar. It turned out to be one of the best Sundays in our church's seventy-five-year history.

Preparing for Loyalty Day

Two months in advance, our church staff and I began to talk about Loyalty Day. At that point we simply wanted to build some initial interest. One month before the event, we began to seriously publicize Loyalty Day. We promoted it in our newsletter every week and announced it in worship services. We explained that Loyalty Day was going to be a day dedicated to reaffirming our loyalty to Christ's church. We encouraged our congregation to express their loyalty to two concrete and tangible ways. We asked them to attend Sunday School and worship and to give a sacrificial offering. Certainly, there is more to loyalty than attendance and giving, but let's not discount these two important elements of commitment.

Two weeks before Loyalty Day, posters appeared throughout the church. We encouraged Sunday School classes to set high attendance goals. We asked teachers to contact every member of their class and encourage them to attend. We created a special order of worship for the occasion. We enlisted several laypersons to lead in the service. Two "old-timers" were asked to prepare testimonies. The choir worked up special music and I wrote a sermon for the occasion called "Expressions of Loyalty."

One week before Loyalty Day, I wrote a letter and mailed it to every member of the church. I spoke about loyalty to Christ and His church. I asked them to attend that Sunday and to give a generous offering. We enclosed a special offering envelope for their use.

Finally, the big day came. Excitement filled the air. Attendance was the best it had been in three years. We brought in the largest one day-offering in the history of the church. A tremendous spirit prevailed in the worship service. Several people made decisions for Christ and His church during the invitation.

We felt the results of Loyalty Day for many months to come. While attendance and giving obviously dropped from the high of that day, it leveled off at a higher average than before. Folks talked about Loyalty Day for a long time. Some suggested that we have one every year or every other year.

An Order of Worship for Loyalty Day

The Worship of God

Loyalty Expressed Trough Praise

Prelude
Choral Call to Worship
Responsive Reading No. 522
Hymn . . . . The Church's One Foundation . . . . No. 236

Loyalty Expressed Through Prayer

Hymn . . . . Sweet Hour of Prayer . . . . No. 401
Discipline of Silence
Pastoral Prayer

Loyalty Expressed Through Testimony

Testimony
Special Music . . . . The Name of Jesus . . . . Men's Quartet
Testimony

Loyalty Expressed Through Proclamation

Choral Anthem . . . . He Lifted Me
Sermon . . . . Expressions of Loyalty . . . . Pastor
Hymn of Invitation . . . . I Surrender All . . . . No. 347

Loyalty Expressed Through Giving

Offertory Hymn . . . . . . Take My Life, and Let It Be . . . . . . No. 373
Offering
Benediction . . . . The Bond of Love

Postlude

Expressions of Loyalty
Prov. 3:3

A pastor once visited the home of one of his church members. When their son saw him outside the storm door he shouted: "Hey Mama! Come quick! The sermon is at the door!"

Well, the sermon is here. I realize, however, that we've already had extra testimonies and music and still have things to do after the sermon, so I'll be brief and to the point.

Today is Loyalty Day, a day to focus our attention on loyalty to our church. Today offers each of us an opportunity to express our loyalty in concrete and tangible ways.

To be loyal means to be faithful. It's not an emotion, although emotional feelings are often part of loyalty. Primarily, loyalty expresses commitment. And commitment is rational, deliberate, and intentional.

I recently heard a remarkable story of loyalty. The story comes from Korea, a place where revival is sweeping the country. It involves a man named Yoon Young Jong. He directs maintenance at a hospital in Pusan and has worked at the hospital for twenty-three years. He is also a deacon at a Baptist church.

Six years ago Mr. Jong's church fell into serious financial problems. The pastor asked the deacons to give sacrificially. Yoon Young Jong is not a wealthy man and was already contributing all he could. So he sold his house and gave the money to the church. For the next few months, he and his family lived in a tent.

During the next winter Mr. Jong cashed in his retirement account to buy a boiler to heat the church building. During the winter months he goes to church two hours early to feed wood into the boiler. He also spends several hours each week sharing his faith with young people and bringing them to Christ and church.

What a remarkable story of loyalty! This man sold his house, cashed in his retirement money, spends hours per week working at the church, and witnesses on a regular basis—that is loyalty!

Today I'm not asking you to sell your house or cash in your IRA. I am, however, asking all of us to seriously evaluate our loyalty to Christ's church. Again and again in the Bible, God tells us to be faithful, committed, and loyal to Jesus and His church.

How do we obey that calling? How can we express our loyalty? Let me briefly share five ways we can express our loyalty to Christ's church.

Positive

First, we can be positive. In Proverbs 17:22 we read, "A cheerful heart is a good medicine, but a downcast spirit dries up the bones."

One way to express loyalty to your church is to be positive. Be optimistic, open to change, and positive about people and programs of the church. Gripes, complaints, and criticism can deeply wound a church.

Perhaps you heard the story about a boy who hitched his dog to the lawn mower and made the dog pull the mower across the grass. A man passed by and the dog stopped to bark. The boy said, "Don't mind the dog; he's just using you as an excuse not to work. It's easier to bark than to pull the mower."

It's easy to bark—to complain and criticize. No church is perfect and no church ever will be. Loyalty, however, demands that we be positive in our attitude, words, and action. We can express loyalty by being positive.

Prayer

Second, we can express our loyalty through prayer. In Colossians 1:9 we read, "We have not ceased to pray for you." Paul assured the church in Colossae that he prayed for them. Prayer is the foundation of a strong church. I'm always encouraged when people tell me they are praying for me and for the church.

Many years ago at Charles Haddon Spurgeon's Tabernacle in London, England, a visitor took a tour of the church facility. Near the end of the tour, the visitor asked to see the power plant of the church. The tour guide took the visitor to the basement and opened the door. The visitor expected to see a huge generator and lots of wires. Instead, he saw 700 people on their knees in prayer. The tour guide said, "This, Sir, is our power plant."

Prayer is the power plant of God's church. If you want to be loyal to this church, pray for her every day.

Presence

Third, we can express loyalty by our presence. The Bible says in Hebrews 10:25, "not neglecting to meet together, as is the habit of some, but encouraging one another."

One of the most visible ways we can be loyal to our church is to be present. We should be here for Bible study, worship, prayer meetings, and special occasions.

It's important for us to be present at church. God wants it, we need it, and it encourages the entire church. Everyone will miss occasionally, but we should be present most of the time.

Participation

A fourth way to express loyalty is through participation. Loyalty demands that we actively participate in the mission and ministry of the church. Being a participant may mean taking a formal position—Sunday School teacher, choir member, and so forth. But everyone, even those who don't have a formal position, can actively participate in the life of the church.

How can we express our loyalty to Christ's church? Four suggestions have been given so far. We can be positive, we can pray, we can be present, and we can participate. Let me mention a final expression of loyalty.

Purse

Finally, we can be loyal with our purse—or our wallet or checkbook. I'm speaking, of course, about being loyal through giving. In 1 Corinthians 16:2 we read, "On the first day of every week, each of you is to put something aside and store it up, as he may prosper."

Financial support is the responsibility of every Christian. I don't talk much about giving from this pulpit but I'm not embarrassed nor hesitant to do so. In His word, God tells us to support the church with our tithes and offerings. How a person spends their money says much about their values and commitment. There is probably no better test of our loyalty than our giving. I hope each of you will seriously consider your level of commitment in the area of giving. God's work cannot be done without your gifts.

In Proverbs 3:3 we read, "Let not loyalty and faithfulness forsake you; bind them about your neck, write them on the tablet of your heart." God wants us to be loyal. Loyal to Him, to His Son Jesus Christ, and to His church.

I'll close today by telling a story from Civil War days. General Sherman was marching into Atlanta, burning homes and destroying the city as he went. In the middle of town lived an elderly lady. She knew about the approach of Sherman's army, but refused to leave her home. When she heard the army marching down her street, destroying everything in their way, she picked a broom—her only weapon—and stood in the middle of the street directly in front of her home. The army stopped when they reached her and a commander spoke to her and tried to move her from the road. "Surely, Madam, you don't think that you can defeat our army by yourself with nothing more than a broomstick."

"No," she replied, "I don't have any illusion that I can win a battle against you. But, when you're through with me, you will know which side I'm on."

Whose side are you on? My prayer is that we'll all be on the side of Christ and His church, and that on this Loyalty Day, we'll renew our commitment to the Lord and to this church.

20

Conservation Sunday

Immediately after graduation from seminary my family and I moved to Augusta, Arkansas, where I pastored the First Baptist Church. Augusta is a small agricultural town with a population of 3,400 people.

A few months after I arrived the county agent dropped by my office. He asked me if I would be willing to observe Soil Conservation Day the following Sunday. He even had bulletin inserts to use for this special Sunday.

I told the county agent that I would consider his request and would call him back in two days. Over the next two days, I struggled with the decision. I'd never heard of Conservation Sunday. Was it a valid enough subject to devote an entire Sunday to its observance? The more I thought about it, however, the more sense it made.

Stewardship of the earth is an important biblical concept. It's also an extremely relevant subject. And in a farming community it certainly made sense to observe such a Sunday.

We observed Conservation Sunday and it proved to be a meaningful service. I'm now convinced that this subject needs to be addressed not only in rural settings but everywhere. Our planet is in trouble. Christian people need to take seriously God's call to be good stewards of His earth. Whether or not you observe Conservation Sunday, this subject needs to be dealt with in your preaching and worship. It's truly a matter of life and death for us and for God's creation.

My guess is that this chapter will be the least-used chapter of this book. Before you overlook it, however, please review the following service and sermon. You don't have to observe Conservation Sunday to use these ideas. The subject matter is important to everybody and is certainly a valid subject to address on Sunday morning.

The Worship of God

I Am the Lord Your God (Hos. 13:4)

Prelude
Choral Call to Worship................... Morning Has Broken
Responsive Reading
    Pastor: I am the Lord your God from the land of Egypt
    People: you know no God but me, and besides me there is no savior.
    Pastor: I am God and not man,
    People: the Holy one in your midst.
Hymn .... All Creatures of Our God and King......... No. 9
Invocation

Hear the Word of the Lord (Hos. 4:1)

Responsive Scripture Reading...................... Hosea 4:1-3
    Leader: Hear the word of the Lord, O people of Israel; for the Lord has
        a controversy with the inhabitants of the land.
    People: There is no faithfulness or kindness, and no knowledge of God
        in the land;
    Leader: there is swearing, lying, killing, stealing, and committing
        adultery;
    People: they break all bounds and murder follows murder.
    Leader: Therefore the land mourns, and all who dwell in it languish,
    People: and also the beasts of the field; and the birds of the air; and
        even the fish of the sea are taken away.
Hymn .... God, Who Stretched the Spangled Heavens..... No. 150
Offering

Therefore the Land Mourns (Hos. 4:3)

Scripture Reading .... Genesis 1:1-5; 2:15
Anthem........................... This Is My Father's World
Sermon .... The Garden

Come, Let Us Return to the Lord (Hos. 6:1)

Invitation Hymn . . . . . God of Earth and Outer Space . . . . . . No. 20
Benediction
Postlude

The Garden
Hos. 4:1-3; 6:1

During seminary years, Paula and I lived in what's called the seminary village. Seminarians affectionately called it "the Gospel Ghetto."

One year we planted a garden in one of the garden plots the seminary provided. We spent many hours tilling, planting, and caring for our garden. From the start, we saw that it was a fine work. The tomato plants grew rapidly, the flowers bloomed, and the beans reached their stalks into the sky. We were proud of our garden and waited in anticipation for the coming fruits of our labor.

One afternoon, however, I received a phone call from a concerned neighbor. She said, "Are you the owners of garden plot number 26?" "Yes," I replied. "I hate to call you" she said, "but some children have sorta messed up your garden. You had better come see it."

We immediately went to the garden. It had been ravished. The tomato plants had been pulled up by their roots, the stakes knocked down, the flowers uprooted, and the beans trampled upon. My wife and I were left with a garden that had been seriously vandalized. We had to make a decision. Fall would arrive before long. Was it too late in the season to start over?

This story is similar to what humanity has done to the environment. Like vandalistic children, we have ravished the garden, earth. Fall is coming soon. Some say it is almost too late to repair the damage. We must act now if we want to save planet earth.

We live today in the midst of an environmental crisis. It is fitting then, to revisit the prophet Hosea, for his warning strikes a familiar ring and has a frightening relevance to our contemporary situation. Let us hear again the Word of God (read Hos. 4:1-3).

Hosea proclaimed that the earth—her land, sky, and seas—were sick.

Why? Because of sin. Sin caused the land to mourn. The birds of the air and the fish of the sea also suffered because of man's sin.

The connection between Hosea's time and ours is obvious. We too, like Israel, have sinned. And our land, its waters and sky, mourns. Because of our irresponsibility, we have threatened the entire planet. Our contemporary situation seems like a fulfillment of the prophesy of Hosea. He speaks of the fish of the sea in anguish. Today much of the water in America is polluted. Our rivers are rapidly becoming running sewers. Even the oceans are threatened. Jacques Cousteau says that the oceans are in danger of dying. Indeed, the fish are in trouble.

Hosea also said that the birds of the sky suffer. Today the birds suffer indeed, as do we, because of air pollution. And now scientists tell us that we are depleting the ozone layer from the atmosphere and that the consequences might be devastating.

Hosea also said that the land and its inhabitants mourn. Today, the land is mourning. Why? Because we poison it. We dump pesticides, nuclear radiation, acid runoff, mercury, phosphates, and herbicides into the land. The chemical pollution of planet earth is a crisis situation. You can't read the paper or watch television without constantly hearing the message that our planet is in serious trouble.

Land, air, and water devastation are only symptoms of a bigger problem. Hosea said the land mourns because the people sin. That certainly describes us. Our greed and irresponsibility threatens the very survival of the planet. Henlee Barnette once said, "If the modern prodigal, the wasteful, polluting spoiler of the earth continues . . . he may well find himself managing an environmental pigsty."

None of us want to destroy the garden. Too much is at stake. Our survival depends on how we respond to the problem. So let's move toward a solution. How do we get out of this mess? The biblical answer is repentance—turning away from sin and towards God who leads us in the right way. Hear again from Hosea, "Come, let us return to the Lord; . . . that he may heal us" (6:1).

God will forgive our sin and healing can come. In our contemporary environmental crisis, how can we be healed? First, we must repent. And that means, at the very least, we will have to change our way of thinking and we will have to change our way of living.

First, we must change our way of thinking.—We desperately need a new theology of creation. For too long, the church has neglected stewardship of the earth. Both conservative and liberal Christianity are at fault. The evangelical church, concerned with personal conversion, has neglected our ecological responsibility to be stewards of the earth. Indeed, many evangelicals are suspicious of environmental efforts. The liberal church, however, has done no better. Their primary efforts have been in the area of human liberation from oppression, thus they also have neglected stewardship of the earth. Both groups have focused exclusively on human life and have forgotten about God's call to tend His garden, to be stewards of His creation.

The Bible, however, is deeply concerned about God's creation. Here is a brief biblical theology of creation.

1. God created the universe. "I am the Lord, who made all things, who stretched out the heavens alone, who spread out the earth" (Isa. 44:24).

2. God affirms His creation. Genesis 1:31 says, "And God saw everything that he had made, and behold, it was very good."

3. God is intimately involved in His creation. "Thou renewest the face of the ground" (Ps. 104:30). "In his hand is the life of every living thing" (Job 12:10). God created the earth and He continues to sustain it.

4. God cares about all life on this planet. We know God cares about people, but He also cares about other life forms. In Leviticus 25 God commanded the people not to overuse the land. In Exodus 23:4-5 God told the people to treat the animals with kindness. In Deuteronomy 20:19-20 we learn that even the trees have rights. "When you beseige a city, . . . you shall not destroy its trees by wielding an axe against them, . . . you shall not cut them down." In Deuteronomy 22 God tells the people not to trap a bird when it is nesting its young. God cares about trees, birds, animals, the land, and all life on our planet.

5. God owns all of creation. The planet is not ours to exploit. In Exodus 19:5 God says, "All the earth is mine." Deuteronomy 10:14 proclaims, "Behold, to the Lord your God belong heaven, . . . the earth with all that

is in it." Psalm 24:1 says, "The earth is the Lord's and the fulness thereof."

6. Sadly, however, we have abused God's creation. Our greed and sin have adversely affected God's world. We just read a vivid example of this truth in today's text, Hosea 4:1-3.

7. God desires renewal for His creation. We see this truth illustrated in Romans 8:21, "Because the creation itself will be set free. . . . the whole creation has been groaning in travail." In Colossians 1 we read that God wants to reconcile to Himself all things, whether on earth or in heaven.

Let me review what I've said. God created this universe. He affirmed the goodness of the creation. He continues to sustain His creation. He cares about all life on the planet. He owns the world. But because of our sin, we've damaged His world. God, however, wants renewal. All of which brings me to a final point.

8. We are called to be responsible stewards of God's creation. In Genesis 2:15 we see that God put mankind in the garden to till it and to keep it. People of faith must be in the business of caring for the planet. One of our God-given roles is to tend the garden.

Second, we must change our way of living. Solving the environmental problem will call for a change in thinking. But it also calls for a change in living. Time does not allow me to get detailed, but we can do much to help the ecology crisis.

First, we must make some changes in our own life-style. Hundreds of small changes could be mentioned. We can drive less and carpool, walk, and ride bikes more. We can work hard at curbing our energy consumption. We can avoid purchasing nonbiodegradable containers and recycle as much as possible. With just a little effort, my family and I have reduced our solid waste disposal by over 50 percent through recycling efforts.

Even more difficult, we need to ask ourselves some hard questions about our materialistic value system. Dorothy Sayers once said, "A society in which consumption has to be artificially stimulated in order to keep production going is a society founded on trash and waste and such a society is a house built upon the sand."[2] We must stop our worship of consumerism if we are to be responsible stewards of the earth. We must take seriously the words of our Lord that you cannot serve both God and money.

It won't be easy, but we can change our life-style. We can slowly learn that bigger isn't always better, that a higher standard of living doesn't buy happiness, and that true peace and contentment come from the simple life which does not take such a toll upon garden earth. So the first step is to make some changes in our life-style.

A second step is to get politically involved as an advocate for the earth. Christianity demands responsible citizenship. Environmental issues are constantly being debated in the government. Write letters to your congressmen and senators demanding ecological responsibility. Get involved in ecological concerns on a local and national basis.

Third, you can join others in the fight to save God's creation. We cannot solve this problem on an individual level. We must work with others. Church groups can be formed for recycling efforts and environmental advocacy. You might also consider joining a regional or national environmental group. These are just a few things we can do, but they are an important beginning.

Hosea told it like it is. Our sin has brought destruction upon the earth. But all is not bleak. Hosea said that healing can come. In order for that to happen, however, we must repent. We need to repent in many areas, but especially in our reckless destruction of the earth. Such repentance calls for a change in our way of thinking and in our way of living. But such changes can bring renewal to the land. Healing can come, God can bandage our wounds and the wounds of the land. Hosea had a vision for a renewed creation. Catch that vision. But remember the reality. The garden has been vandalized. Fall will be here soon. Let us act now before it is too late.

Note

1. Quoted in Henlee H. Barnette, *The Church and the Ecological Crisis* (Grand Rapids: William B. Eerdman's Publishing Co., 1972), 47.